JAMES N. LAPSLEY is Associate Profes.
of Pastoral Theology, Princeton Theolog.
cal Seminary. He is a graduate of South-
western University, Union Theological
Seminary in Virginia, University of Chicago Divinity School (Ph.D.). He was also
a Fellow in Theology and Psychiatry, Menninger Foundation.

SALVATION AND HEALTH

SALVATION AND HEALTH

THE INTERLOCKING
PROCESSES OF LIFE

by
JAMES N. LAPSLEY

THE WESTMINSTER PRESS

Philadelphia

Scripture quotations from the Revised Standard Version of the Bible are copyright, 1946 and 1952, by the Division of Christian Education of the National Council of Churches, and are used by permission.

ISBN 0–664–20936–X

Library of Congress Catalog Card No. 79–188383

BOOK DESIGN BY
DOROTHY ALDEN SMITH

Published by The Westminster Press ®
Philadelphia, Pennsylvania

PRINTED IN THE UNITED STATES OF AMERICA

Library of Congress Cataloging in Publication Data

Lapsley, James N
Salvation and health.

Includes bibliographical references.
1. Salvation. 2. Hygiene. 3. Mental hygiene.
I.Title.
BT732.L33   234   79-188383
ISBN 0-664-20936-X

For Brenda

Contents

FOREWORD   9

I. THE CHURCH'S CONCEPTUAL
   CREDIBILITY GAP   15

II. HISTORY OF THE SALVATION-HEALTH
    RELATIONSHIP   31

III. THE CONTEMPORARY SITUATION   46

IV. A DYNAMIC PROCESS MODEL
    FOR RELATING SALVATION AND HEALTH   86

V. IMPLICATIONS OF THE MODEL
   FOR THEOLOGICAL ANTHROPOLOGY   122

VI. IMPLICATIONS FOR MINISTRY   144

INDEX   173

Foreword

The thesis of this book is that a careful examination of the concept of salvation in the Christian faith in relation to a viable contemporary view of health can provide the basic clue to the most acute question facing the church today—its lack of understanding of man. The want of a sound anthropology is one of the roots of the crisis in which the church finds itself today, if it is not indeed the main source of that crisis, as I shall contend. For despite radical advances in the scientific study of man, the church continues to limp along with outworn notions inherited from the past.

Not that the church has nothing to contribute to a viable understanding of man, however. Indeed, I shall contend that the conception of salvation in the tradition—long a stumbling block for many and a scandal for others who smile nervously at the revivalist's question, "Are you saved?"—can itself provide the basic tool for such an understanding when interpreted in the light of recent developments in theology.

It will also be contended that this is not merely or even primarily an academic matter of interest to professional theologians. An understanding of the relationship between salvation and health is vital for the working theology of ministers —or what I shall call *professional theology* in the sense that it provides the basic conceptual tools which are needed to guide a responsible ministry. Professional theology in this sense does not mean a set of abstractions behind which a minister can hide when the going gets rough, but rather precisely the basic principles by means of which he understands his situation and responsibly acts within it. Central to this understanding is an adequate conception of man.

There are three strands of thinking that have been woven together in producing this book. The first is an interest in the question of health and especially of mental health, which began in a formal sense in the spring of 1958 when I was attempting to formulate a dissertation proposal with the help of Perry D. LeFevre, then on the Federated Theological Faculty of the University of Chicago, now dean of the Chicago Theological Seminary. LeFevre introduced me to the complexity of the subject but encouraged me to pursue it, which I did in my dissertation. The following year, Paul W. Pruyser of the Menninger Foundation, Topeka, Kansas, offered a seminar at Chicago on the theme of health, which further stimulated and challenged me. During the academic year 1960–1961, I was a Fellow in Theology and Psychiatric Theory at the Menninger Foundation, where I continued my interest in and pursuit of the health question with the help and encouragement of the late Thomas W. Klink, Pruyser, Seward Hiltner, and Herbert Klemmer, who served as my psychiatric adviser. Out of these experiences grew the Salvation and Health course at Princeton Theological Seminary, offered since 1963, within which the principal ideas found in this book took essentially their present form.

The second strand of thinking involved is that of process theology, which also dates to the spring of 1958, when I audited a course at Chicago by Bernard M. Loomer and Bernard E. Meland entitled "The Status of Empirical Theology." Up until that time I had not imagined that it had status at all, so what I found in that course constituted a kind of minor revelation—the discovery of a tradition in theology about which I knew almost nothing. The concerns of the course were by no means restricted to process theology, as Professor Me-

land has never identified himself with that movement, but it
whetted my appetite for more. At the same time I was serving as a Student Chaplain in Billings Hospital of the University
of Chicago Clinics, and for a time had as my "parish" the
hematology section, in which many persons were slowly dying of cancers of the circulatory and lymphatic systems. I had
great difficulty in reconciling this mass confrontation with pain,
suffering, and death with traditional conceptions of the benev-
olence and power of God, and slowly began to see that the
view of God in process thought as more limited in power, and
evil as the result of the "mutual obstructiveness" of things,
offered a powerful way of understanding what was hap-
pening and of enhancing my ministry to those who were suffering. Since that time, process theology has become the subject of several important volumes (at that time the work of
Charles Hartshorne was virtually alone in the field) by such
theologians as John B. Cobb, Jr., Daniel Day Williams, and
Schubert Ogden, and my interest in it has continued to grow,
though I have published nothing of my own that has touched
it in more than a peripheral way. I believe it holds the key to
a viable theology for ministry in our time, despite some genuine problems, and offer this present volume as a contribution
to theological anthropology in the process mode.

The third strand concerns method in theology, and in particular methods of relating traditional materials with those
which have traditionally been outside the field of theology,
particularly the sciences of man. In my doctoral dissertation,
"The Devotional Life and Mental Health" (1961), I developed
a way of correlating theological, philosophical, and scientific
perspectives which I have continued to pursue. Based upon the
work of Susanne K. Langer and Daniel Day Williams, this
methodological approach focused upon three interrelated modes
of knowing as essential to theology. The first of these was
called *presentational*, in that it contains essentially the intui-
tive and mythic elements in the Christian tradition. It is the
Judeo-Christian story of salvation; it is not subject to refuta-

tion or verification by logical and empirical procedures, though some aspects of it can be clarified by discursive reason. Hence the second mode of knowing is *discursive*, in which aspects of the Christian story can be logically clarified, such as in the development of theories of atonement, though these aspects cannot be either verified or refuted. The third mode of knowing (and here I went beyond Williams and Langer) I called *empirical*, in the broad sense of the term as referring to direct experience of some kind, not in the narrow sense of following some agreed-upon rules of mathematics or logic, though this is included. Here it is possible to confirm or refute some aspects of theology, as through archaeological investigation or clinical research into the nature of man's psyche. We know rather certainly, for instance, that whatever sin is, it cannot be equated with conscious intentions as some of our forefathers were wont to do. The personality is too complex to allow for that.

Though these modes can be isolated and treated separately to some extent, as I have been doing above, in doing theology they all occur in an interrelated matrix of discussion in which they are seen to be mutually influencing one another. For instance, archaeological and geological evidence combined to make the literal interpretation of the six days of creation untenable, even though this evidence did not compel disbelief in creation per se. Modern evidence about the development of moral values throws into question a penal theory of atonement, though it does not compel disbelief in the need for atonement and that it has been accomplished in principle through the events cited in the Christian story. Thus it is that these modes of knowing affect one another significantly, and evidence from the empirical mode may influence conceptualizing at the discursive level and even our understanding of the basic presentational story.

In this volume these relationships will be seen to be taking place at many points in the discussion, particularly in Chapter V, where the implications of the model for relating salvation and health are spelled out. They will not be labeled as such, since that would be tedious, but the reader is invited to see for himself.

This book is written primarily for ministers in the parish and in other settings in which they are engaged in direct ministry to persons and groups, though I hope it will be of interest to theologians as well. The text was composed with ministers in mind in particular. The notes at the end of each chapter serve two purposes in addition to documentation. For those who wish to investigate a particular topic further, additional reading is occasionally suggested, and there are some technical discussions that may be of interest mostly to specialists in the several theological disciplines.

In addition to encouraging me to develop the line of thought represented in these pages, Seward Hiltner has rendered invaluable editorial help with the manuscript. Daniel L. Migliore has also carefully read it and offered useful suggestions, particularly in the sections dealing with modern theology. To them go my deepest thanks, though the final responsibility for the text, of course, rests with me.

My thanks also go to Elaine Apple, who typed the manuscript and cheerfully and competently endured with me the revising and correctional process that such enterprises entail.

J. N. L.

Princeton, New Jersey

Chapter I

The Church's
Conceptual Credibility Gap

1. Crisis

That we have a crisis in the church is not news to anyone who has been in it, or even around it, during the past decade. Evidences of this are not wanting. We have only to look at the statistics depicting decline in attendance at worship and in giving to church causes beyond the local level.[1] But if it is a truism that the church faces a crisis, it is by no means so clear what the nature of the crisis is.

To some observers who have been vocal for at least two decades, it is due to the failure of the church to face responsibly its prophetic task in relation to a society characterized by affluence and indifference on the one hand, and poverty and injustice on the other. To some more recent observers, however, just the reverse seems to be the case, in that the gap between prophetic clergy and conservative lay persons with vested interests in the *status quo* has grown so wide that the result has been demoralizing to many, and has goaded others into retaliatory action in the form of organizations of "concerned" laymen who hope to diminish, if not extinguish, the power of the clergy in the churches.[2]

Another approach to understanding the crisis in the church is that of laying it to the emotional instability of the clergy in their demanding roles. This was particularly widespread in the 1950's, and produced a battery of research on ministers which attempted in one way or another to discover what was wrong with them, and sometimes to prescribe a cure.[3]

Still others have pointed to the recent upheavals in the culture as a whole, and suggested that the churches, as part of the culture, and especially as value-carrying institutions in it, are deeply affected by these upheavals. Certainly it is true that changing personal, sexual, and marital patterns have involved the churches in increasing uncertainty and some confusion about these matters. Further, the extreme mobility of persons in our culture is antithetical to the parochial system upon which the church structure is based, and the church has so far found no really successful way of coping with this mobility and the lack of rootedness needed for commitment.

While all these factors are, I believe, involved in the present crisis, they are not sufficient to explain the long, gradual (though with many peaks and valleys) decline in relevance, significance, and influence of the church. This decline has been going on for much longer than any of the factors mentioned above. As Philip Rieff has said, the church is "a great and dying patient" of the sociologist of religion, such as Rieff, who sees no substitute for it as the bearer of the values of the culture.[4] While we are not concerned here with the precise analysis of all the factors in this decline, it is important to emphasize that it is not of recent origin, dating at least to the eighteenth century and the age of the Enlightenment, if not before.

To be sure, the decline in attendance and giving mentioned earlier is of rather recent origin, since World War II touched off an important revival of interest in religion, at least in the United States. Nevertheless, this current decline, especially since it appears to involve precisely the central transmitters of value—young adults with children—appears to be a continuation of what Matthew Arnold once described as the "melancholy, long withdrawing roar" of the tide of faith.[5]

Some observers and "physicians to the church," while perhaps conceding that the decline is real and of long duration, nevertheless contend that it is not a full-scale crisis, because of some current signs of life in the church. Among these are Seward Hiltner and George W. Webber, who, while taking very different points of view about the nature of these signs, nevertheless agree that they are present.[6] Clinical pastoral education has been pioneering in creative education methods with seminarians and ministers for more than forty years, while newer forms of "action" training in urban work match it in boldness of approach if not always in sophistication. The emphasis on lay participation, which is becoming more than lip service designed to placate restive laymen, is another such sign, and others could doubtless be named.

Although I agree that these are genuine signs of vitality, and especially concur with Hiltner's thesis that the difficulties of the minister's role and his personal debility have been considerably exaggerated, and that much current "ferment" in the ministry may be creative, still it appears that the general picture of decline will continue and accelerate unless some basic problems are dealt with. For, in my opinion, and as a central presupposition of this book, none of these positive signs really touches the heart of the matter. They deal with significant aspects of the church's life, but at the core of that life is a near vacuum of conceptual structure that has led the church dangerously close to caving in upon itself. There is no underlying and unifying understanding of what the church can be and should be about in the world. Specifically, there is no viable understanding of man and his destiny—viable in the sense of being genuinely adequate for the needs of the church in its situation. There has not been such a theological anthropology adequate for its time in at least two hundred years, and perhaps longer.

2. Theory and Practice

It is a commonplace notion, but a true one nonetheless, that without a good theory one cannot consistently have good practice. Occasionally, one may perform well or even spectacularly on the basis of a poor theory or no theory at all, and may even survive indefinitely on that basis, if the expectations of one's clientele are not too high. For instance, medicine survived for centuries on theories now regarded as patent nonsense, on the basis of the placebo effect and occasional lucky remedies, because the level of expectation was generally low (though in individual cases paradoxically high to achieve the placebo effect, in which the doctor gives the patient a remedy to please him, and the patient gets better to please the doctor).[7] It was not until the seventeenth century that medicine began to be practiced on what we now think of as a scientific basis.

Today we have learned to have high expectations of practice of all sorts through advancements in science and technology. Though such expectations may sometimes be unrealistic or downright illusory, they are met often enough to sustain the high level. In the church we find that not only do people have great difficulty in stating what their expectations are, but that the church has no coherent concrete expectations of itself in relation to people. It remains content to state its goal either in very abstract terms such as helping people to be more loving or else in metaphorical language like "bringing in the Kingdom of God." These phrases may be meaningful to some, but to many they have no meaning at all.

A still more serious aspect of the problem is that, apart from his communicating theology, most ministers have no professional theology or fundamental theory about their work, and do not even recognize the need for such a theory. One of the liabilities of the Protestant Reformation was that its extreme emphasis on preaching created the impression that a minister had no need for any theology that "wouldn't preach." While a part of the intent of this idea was to prevent the minister from engaging in speculative thinking that had no relation to his work, an unfortunate side effect created the impression that he needed no theory about what to do if it lacked homiletical merit.

While genuinely coherent "practical theology" that is more than a hodgepodge of hints and that helps to draw from diverse secular sources is beginning to be available through the work of Seward Hiltner and others, these attempts are principally frameworks within which the minister can understand and organize his work.[8] They assume that the minister has already a viable understanding of man which he can fit into the framework, which then gives the handles that he needs for decision-making. Though the emergence of practical theology in the modern sense has greatly helped some ministers and their churches to a more coherent and meaningful ministry, it still leaves largely unanswered the more basic question about man, and hence is of limited usefulness. In short, it can show a minister *how* to make decisions, including what the options may be and the processes involved in decision-making, but cannot show him *what* the criteria for deciding are. It is a map, but the traveler must decide somehow where he wants to go before he consults the map. In practice, consulting the map may result in modification of the destination, and that may happen in pastoral practice as well. But the need for a clear idea of the realities he confronts in dealing with his people and of the possibilities and limits set by those realities is nevertheless a basic necessity for ministers, but one that he typically does without.

Hence this book is addressed focally to shedding light on this question of the realities and possibilities of relating to persons and groups of persons in the church. As important as a theology for communication to persons is, it is basically derivative from a more comprehensive theory of man in his relationship to God which must be foundational for all operations of ministry. We shall be discussing such a constructive view of man later in detail, but first a brief examination of the failure of theological anthropology during the past two centuries is in order, in the light of my prior assertion that the current crisis in the church goes at least that far back.

3. The Failure of Theological Anthropology

The Protestant Reformation and the subsequent Counter-Reformation in the Catholic Church took place as the end of

20 SALVATION AND HEALTH

the Middle Ages and the rise of modern nation-states pro-
foundly shook the social and cultural patterns of northern
Europe. Luther's doctrine of justification by faith alone proved
to be an answer to the uncertainty of large numbers of persons
caught in the grip of these changes, which, coupled with the
plague and almost constant warfare (beginning to be modern
in the sense of involving whole populations rather than only
a few professionals) produced an atmosphere of terror per-
vading everyday life. The corollary doctrine of election, held
but not emphasized by Luther, was to become an additional
bulwark against evil within and without in the thought of
Calvin and his followers.

As the seventeenth century finally brought an end to the
Reformation period and its religiously oriented wars with the
Peace of Westphalia in 1648, so it also brought the beginnings
of the Enlightenment and modern science. Luminaries such
as Newton and Galileo began to show that our planet is only
a small part of a vast scheme of nature operating by apparently
fixed and predetermined law. Theology responded with Scho-
lastic debates over the nature of the Fall and the decrees of
God, with the orthodox Calvinists finally opting for views that
placed all of life in the category of results of decisions made
by God in his remote and inscrutable will. Whatever the logical
merits of this position, it now appears to have been a part of
the "baroque style" defense against the new anxiety generated by the demonstration of man's smallness and isolation.[9]
The price of this was, of course, to make man into a puppet
totally controlled by forces natural and supernatural beyond
his own ken.

This was the situation as the eighteenth century opened.
In 1703 both John Wesley and Jonathan Edwards were born.
Each contributed mightily to the great revivals of the eighteenth century, and in his own way attempted to develop a
theological anthropology suited for his time. However, both
ultimately failed, though Wesley's emphasis on "heart" religion
produced indirectly a near revolution in the lives of the English

working classes, and Edwards almost succeeded in building a comprehensive and relevant doctrine of man.

Wesley's failure was in his lack of interest in relating his understanding of man to the developing scientific world view, and in his relative neglect of the social and communal dimensions of man's life, though he emphasized small groups for the nurture of the individual. His emphasis on the emotional life of man, though not wrong in itself, made it difficult to build bridges to intellectual and corporate dimensions of life. Methodists have subsequently tended to dichotomize personal and social concerns. The latter have often been present among them, but without integral connection to the core of Wesley's anthropology.[10]

Edwards, on the other hand, strove for a balanced view of man and took both head and heart dimensions seriously, feeling compelled by the evidence of the Great Awakening to accept "enthusiasm" as a genuine part of the work of the Holy Spirit, though not a primary or distinguishing mark. Further, he took seriously the philosophy and science of his day, and developed his view of man partly on the basis of Locke's epistemology. Yet Edwards, too, failed to deal adequately with the corporate and political side of the life of man and remained preoccupied with the individual's relationship to God. A planned systematic theology, not really begun at the time of his death, might well have remedied this problem, such was Edwards' grasp. As it was, the profounder dimensions of his work left little impression on his immediate heirs, while the more sensational aspects of his sermons have branded him as a fiery and vindictive Puritan.[11]

After the Kantian revolution in philosophy at the end of the eighteenth century seemed to make all traditional discussion of transcendence obsolete, the great German theologian F. D. E. Schleiermacher built a brilliant attempt at overcoming this problem on the religious experience of the individual himself, viewed as a feeling of absolute dependence. But, though Schleiermacher emphasized the emotional side of man's life,

he was not anti-intellectual, and was thoroughly conversant
with the best his culture had to offer. In the early years of
the nineteenth century, however, modern psychology had not
even been born, so that this dimension of Schleiermacher's
treatment of man was primitive in its understanding of the
phenomenon of consciousness—a key concept in his position.
Moreover, he did not succeed, as Wesley had not, in developing a view of man's social relations in the world which was
integral to his position, though he was not unconcerned with
this problem.[12]

Schleiermacher is regarded as the father of modern liberal
theology, and his successors in this tradition generally followed
his position on the matters in focus here. Paradoxically, the
more orthodox and conservative theologians, however much
they differed on other issues, presented anthropology in much
the same dichotomized way (soul-body) that the liberals did,
except for more emphasis on sin and man's inability to save
himself. They also tended to compartmentalize the life of man
into thinking, feeling, and willing compartments, and were
even more prone, of course, to build walls between man's
private, individual (spiritual) world, and his social, political,
and economic (secular) world.

Walter Rauschenbusch saw the folly of this dichotomy in the
early days of this century, and strove desperately to overcome
it. Though he is usually regarded as emphasizing the social
gospel to the exclusion of the individual, even a casual perusal
of his writings clearly shows that he was also concerned about
persons as individuals. His vision was that of whole persons
participating in a healed society. Only in his failure to understand the complexities of human personality and interaction,
which resulted in what today appears to be a somewhat naïve
estimate of the capacity of the individual for wholeness and
of the malleability of corporate structures, did Rauschenbusch
miss the mark.[13] His is the primary precursor of the position
to be set forth in this book.

Reinhold Niebuhr did understand much of the complexity of
human relationships and the paradoxes of human motivation.

Further, he clearly saw that the injustices of society were not easily righted, even if individual intentions were relatively unambiguous. Indeed, Niebuhr emphasized the paradoxes and contradictions of human nature to such an extent that his position is not really useful as a guide to constructive continuing relationships in parish or other settings, however much it may inspire to prophetic action in a clear-cut crisis. Toward the end of his career, Niebuhr began to move toward a more positive position regarding the possibilities of individual development in an open society, but this emphasis was left as a hope rather than a fully wrought out position.[14]

The two acknowledged giants of twentieth-century theology, Karl Barth and Paul Tillich, did not in my opinion contribute greatly to anthropology. Though differing widely on questions of method and the understanding of God and his relationship to the world, both saw man as bound by sin and contradiction. For them, theology was a protest against the dehumanization of man in the twentieth century. Both were heavily influenced by existentialist thinking (though Barth disavowed it) which pictured man in existence as alienated from his true nature and confronted by a hostile environment challenging him to decision in moment-by-moment encounters as response to grace. However valuable this might be for self-understanding, especially in time of great crisis and upheaval, it does not offer much to those who must necessarily be concerned about the continuities of life as well as the discontinuities.[15]

Though the modern thinkers mentioned generally overcame the crudely dualistic dichotomies that characterized the orthodox tradition—body and soul, individual and society, sacred and secular—they did not offer a fully viable anthropology because of their failure to understand how the dynamics of personality operate in relationships, and because they lacked a comprehensive grasp of the reality of nature of which man is a part. Despite good intentions, their views of man tended always to be one-sided in emphasis, disconnected, and vague and misleading at crucial points.

Today we do have a better model of how the human being

actually functions, and we have a framework within which to set it. In what has come to be called psychoanalytic ego psychology we have the essentials for a dynamic understanding of persons in relationship, and in process philosophy we have the framework. Neither of these is a perfect instrument, but in my judgment they are potent enough in combination to provide the needed revitalization of Christian themes about man in a way concrete enough to have direct relevance to ministry.

4. Salvation and Health

In order to deal with a problem as big as this one, some conceptual handles must be found around which to organize the material. I have chosen the relationship between salvation and health as the focal concern of this effort, in the belief that a careful analysis of this relationship and construction on that basis of a model for understanding man in community provides the key to anthropology. In the themes of salvation and health we find Biblical, traditional, and modern scientific norms for man juxtaposed. By attempting to understand man from this normative perspective we avoid the reductionism of pathological and negative approaches, and the false claim of scientific objectivity in "descriptive" approaches. In dealing with man, one must acknowledge the perspective that one is taking; there is no complete objectivity. There is some danger in taking a normative approach that the darker side of man's existence, his sin and destructiveness, his weakness and frailty, will be slighted. Hence, special care will be taken to show the scope and role of such factors.

First, we shall explore the history of the relationship between salvation and health from the earliest Biblical accounts to the present time. Then an examination in some detail will be made of how some contemporary theologians have handled the relationship, either directly or indirectly. Then my own model for relating the two as interlocking processes will be presented, and finally the implications of this model for theological anthropology and its application to problems of ministry will be discussed.

In seeking to employ process philosophy and psychoanalytic ego psychology as important tools, along with some others in theology and the sciences, I am aware of important criticisms directed at both of these, as well as at all speculative philosophy and dynamic psychology in general.[16] Further, I know the general opinion among theologians that too close linkage with any secular framework is deadly for theology, since it makes theology time-bound to the particular epoch in which these frameworks are operating. My response to this cogent point is simply to accept the risks, because I have no alternative other than to work with the best available in my time, knowing that my work will not last forever. But it is not meant to last forever. It is for today and tomorrow. If it speaks to them, it will have made its contribution to the distant future as a part of its legacy. That these intellectual tools will continue to be meaningful pointers toward reality for the near future is the calculated risk which I accept.

Some readers, while accepting the idea that the conceptual credibility gap in the church lies behind much of its current crisis, may wonder why a faulty notion of man is said to be the culprit, rather than the doctrine of God, which has been so often focal in the past. Basically, this is because those in the church are men, and lack of understanding of their problems and possibilities is a disastrous impediment. Already, several able men have begun to develop the doctrine of God from a process point of view, notably Charles Hartshorne, John B. Cobb, Jr., Daniel Day Williams, and Schubert Ogden. So far their efforts have not extended very far into the area of anthropology, though Williams' book, *The Spirit and the Forms of Love*,[17] has touched important aspects of it. I do not believe their important work will get a hearing in the church at large unless a meaningful anthropology can be elaborated which could then be linked to the wider theological spectrum.

Finally, ours is a day of a new, if chastened, humanism. Men everywhere are reaching out for new possibilities for developing their potential and enjoying its fruits. This mood has extended to the church, as Roger L. Shinn in his stimulating volume, in the series New Directions in Theology Today, entitled *Man: The New Humanism*[18] clearly shows. He also makes clear that the church still has more questions than answers about man, which is an added challenge for this present work. I think we can begin to tip the scale in favor of answers.

NOTES

1. Some churches are still showing signs of growth, of course, especially Pentecostal churches. In speaking about the church, I have in mind primarily the "main line" churches through which major aspects of our culture have been transmitted. This is not to say that the churches that are growing are not significant, but that their rate of growth will probably be slowed as they move upward on the socioeconomic ladder to encounter the same problems that have beset middle-class churches.

2. Jeffery K. Hadden, *The Gathering Storm in the Churches* (Doubleday & Company, Inc., 1969), p. 6 *et passim.* Hadden's central thesis is "that the Protestant Churches are involved in a deep and entangling crisis which in the years ahead may seriously disrupt or alter the very nature of the church" (*ibid.*, p. 5). He sees this crisis as one having three dimensions: (*a*) purpose and meaning, (*b*) belief, and (*c*) authority. In his book he emphasizes the first as being focal to the cleavage between clergy and laity, with the others contributing to it. I think that Hadden is substantially correct in his thesis, though the implications of what he calls the crisis of belief are even more significant than he suggests, since it is the source of fundamental confusion. His careful documentation and analysis will repay any reader concerned about the church.

3. Most of this research is available in abstracts published by Robert J. Menges and James E. Dittes, *Psychological Studies of Clergymen: Abstracts of Research* (Thomas Nelson & Sons, 1965).

4. This comment was made by Rieff following a public lecture at Princeton Theological Seminary, May, 1967.

5. Matthew Arnold, "Dover Beach," in Paul R. Lieder, Robert M. Lovett, and Robert K. Root (eds.), *British Poetry and Prose* (Houghton Mifflin Company, 1938), Vol. II, p. 680.

6. Hiltner's volume, *Ferment in the Ministry* (Abingdon Press, 1969), offers a strong case for the viability of the role of parish minister for those with enough flexibility, strength, and imagination. Webber, in several publications based on his experience in East Harlem in New York City, has stressed commitment through group social action and Bible study, e.g., *The Congregation in Mission* (Abingdon Press, 1964).

7. Arthur K. Shapiro, "A Contribution to the History of the Placebo Effect," *Journal of the Behavioral Sciences*, Vol. V (1960), pp. 109–135.

8. Seward Hiltner, *Preface to Pastoral Theology* (Abingdon Press, 1958). Hiltner proposed a perspectival model of ministry with three perspectives—shepherding, communicating, and organizing—seen as interrelated on the basis of "field theory." Recently, Coval B. MacDonald has suggested a modification of this approach on the basis of general systems theory in the essay entitled "Methods of Study in Pastoral Theology," in William B. Oglesby, Jr. (ed.), *The New Shape of Pastoral Theology* (Abingdon Press, 1969), pp. 164–178.

9. Edward A. Dowey in a personal communication. Dowey is a specialist in the theology of the Reformation and post-Reformation periods.

10. In dealing thus briefly with so complex and important a figure as Wesley, as is the case with each theologian touched in this section, I am admittedly running some risks of distorting his position and impact. Undoubtedly some important nuances have been neglected altogether. Nevertheless, for the purpose of getting some overview of the modern history of theological anthropology among Protestants, I believe my procedure to be sound. For a perceptive contemporary treatment of Wesley's more central writings, see Albert C. Outler's *John Wesley* (Oxford University Press, 1964).

11. Edwards remained squarely within the Calvinist tradition, emphasizing the depravity of man and the sovereign power and grace of God in contrast to Wesley, who held more moderate

views on both points. Though these were theoretical differences often emphasized in the theological struggles of the past two centuries, their consequences do not appear to have been so important for the practice of ministry as those mentioned in the text. Edwards' complete works, the only comprehensive guide to his thinking, have not been republished in this century, and are difficult to find in good condition (*The Works of President Edwards*, ed. by Sereno Dwight, 10 vols.; S. Converse, 1829). Conrad Cherry has recently published *The Theology of Jonathan Edwards* (Doubleday & Company, Inc., 1966), a good introduction to his thought. Perry Miller's *Jonathan Edwards* (Meridian Books, Inc., The World Publishing Company, 1959) may be read for striking illumination of some aspects of Edwards' thought, though its general thesis that Edwards was primarily a philosopher and only a theologian by accident of history is strained.

12. See F. D. E. Schleiermacher, *The Christian Faith*, tr. and ed. by H. R. Mackintosh and J. S. Stewart (Edinburgh: T. & T. Clark, 1928). This is Schleiermacher's systematic theology. Essentially he followed Luther's position regarding the church and the world, viewing the former as "subsisting" as an alien in the latter (*ibid.*, pp. 582 ff.). Though this dichotomizing tendency was mitigated by his broad sympathies and interests, it persisted in the individualism of later liberal theology.

13. See Walter Rauschenbusch, *A Theology for the Social Gospel* (The Macmillan Company, 1917), Ch. X.

14. Niebuhr's central work is *The Nature and Destiny of Man* (Charles Scribner's Sons, 1949). The movement toward a more positive view of man in society is found in *Man's Nature and His Communities* (Charles Scribner's Sons, 1965), pp. 109–119.

15. Like Niebuhr, both Barth and Tillich moved toward more appreciation of human possibilities in the latter stages of their careers. This was more obviously so in the case of Barth, whose essay *The Humanity of God* shocked the theological world in 1956, and was translated into English by John Newton Thomas and Thomas Wieser (John Knox Press, 1960). The third of the three volumes of Tillich's *Systematic Theology* (The University of Chicago Press, 1963) appears in some ways to go beyond his earlier position in affirming that the capacity of man for love

and spiritual existence is maintained (*ibid.*, pp. 111–137). Despite these shifts, however, Barth's Christocentric anthropology and Tillich's existential anthropology remained centered on man's fragmented character as departure from an ideal norm, and as such envision his partial and apparently sporadic response to grace and consequent liberty and fellowship (Barth) or participation in the New Being (Tillich). See Karl Barth, *Church Dogmatics,* tr. and ed. by G. T. Thomson, G. W. Bromiley, T. F. Torrance *et al.,* 4 vols. (Edinburgh: T. & T. Clark, 1936–1960), III, 2, pp. 55–285, and IV, 3, pp. 664 ff.; and Paul Tillich, *Systematic Theology,* Vol. II, pp. 59–78, 165 ff.

16. Though most of the criticism of "metaphysics" has been directed toward one particular type, namely, idealistic metaphysics, there have been some specific criticisms of process philosophy (in addition to the one which I share that Whitehead and his followers have not always stated clearly what they meant) of which perhaps the two following are most cogent: (*a*) It is actually a modified form of idealism, and hence shares in the same defects pointed out in all idealisms—their abstract character and failure to show adequately the relationship between appearance and reality. I hold that, though there is an undeniable idealistic element in process philosophy (the doctrine of eternal objects), it is better called an idealistic naturalism than a naturalistic idealism. Its roots in modern physics prevent it from ever losing its central concern with the concreteness of events. For an illuminating discussion of this issue, see John B. Cobb, Jr., *A Christian Natural Theology Based on the Thought of Alfred North Whitehead* (The Westminster Press, 1965), pp. 150–175. (*b*) By emphasizing reality as process, event, and occasion, the discontinuities of reality are obscured, and one "thing" merges into another without any definable distinction being possible. I think this is a genuine difficulty for theologians who attempt to use process philosophy, for it has implications for the God-man relationship as well as for the understanding of history as involving discontinuity as well as continuity. I think this issue can be dealt with, and I shall discuss it in some detail in Chapter V.

The most compelling criticism of psychoanalytic ego psychology from within dynamic psychology is that it does not take the category of relationship seriously, and sticks to the intrapsychic aspects of personality in too objective a fashion. This has been pressed by the *enfant terrible* of British psychiatry, R. D. Laing, in telling fashion in his *The Politics of Experience* (Ballantine Books, Inc., 1967), pp. 49–50. I think that this is essentially true but that it is remediable by placing ego psychology within a process framework that puts great emphasis on experience and relationship. The reader must judge by this book whether I am right.

The other criticism of ego psychology, less serious, is that it is really a hybrid, pretending allegiance to Freud but actually more like "fulfillment models" in psychology which emphasize self-actualization and hold that not all behavior is defensive. See Salvatore R. Maddi, *Personality Theories: A Comparative Analysis* (The Dorsey Press, Inc., 1968), p. 43, for a lucid discussion of this issue. I think the point is correct, but that it is not a serious problem. Ego psychology derives from Freud's position, but has been modified in the light of subsequent clinical and research experience, especially with children.

Discussion of critiques of dynamic psychology in general are reserved for Chapter III, where they will be dealt with in the text.

17. Daniel Day Williams, *The Spirit and the Forms of Love* (Harper & Row, Publishers, Inc., 1968).
18. Roger L. Shinn, *Man: The New Humanism,* Vol. VI of New Directions in Theology Today, 7 vols., ed. by William Hordern (The Westminster Press, 1968).

Chapter II

History of the
Salvation-Health Relationship

1. The Old Testament

For those of us who came of age in the 1940's and 1950's—
and perhaps for some of us since then—it may come as a surprise to discover that the central foci of these terms in the Old
Testament do not mean the same thing at all, nor do they even
refer to the same kinds of events. In the era ended in the
1960's it was widely thought that distinctions between these
terms were largely a matter of unimportant technicalities (even
while some more traditionally oriented Christians thought there
was no relationship at all, lest the state of the body affect the
soul in some basic way). In the Old Testament there is a
relationship, but not a close one.

The Old Testament conception of salvation is derived primarily from the great event of Israel's deliverance from Egypt
in the exodus. Thus the terms for "salvation," *yeshua* and
yasha, are derived from the verb root that means to deliver
safely to a place of ease and peace. The flight from Egypt and
the ultimate entry into the Promised Land, whatever their
status as history, formed the core of the image of salvation.
This image was communal, this-worldly, and envisioned the
distress from which deliverance was needed as primarily external to the people of Israel. Each of these elements was
modified in the course of the history of the Hebrew people

during the long period covered by the Old Testament and the Apocrypha, but none entirely disappeared.

The *communal* character of salvation was closely related to the basic understanding of man in corporate rather than individual terms. God's covenant was with the Hebrew people, not with individual Hebrews. Only by participation in the life of the clan, tribe, and nation did the individual find identity and meaning. This is clearly seen not only in the meaning of the original exodus events and the conquest of the Promised Land, but with equal vividness in the prophecies of Deutero-Isaiah, the prophet of the exile in Babylon who foresaw the return of the Israelites to Jerusalem: "Behold, the Lord has proclaimed to the end of the earth: Say to the daughter of Zion, 'Behold, your salvation comes'" (Isa. 62:11). This communal conception continued to dominate Jewish thinking down to the period of the New Testament in the growth of apocalyptic prophecy which foresaw the decisive intervention of God in a climactic holocaust at the end of history in which the reign of God through his people would finally be established (Isa., chs. 24 to 27; Dan., chs. 7 to 12; Zech., chs. 12 to 14).

Within this overarching view, however, an emphasis on the individual and his personal needs and worth developed, in some degree of tension with the dominant corporate motif. This view is represented by the Wisdom Literature and some of the psalms, as in Ps. 27: "The Lord is my light and my salvation; whom shall I fear?" (Ps. 27:1). The concept of salvation itself does not play a significant role in the Wisdom Literature, rather the central concern is to get wisdom (*chokmah*). It is perhaps significant, however, that the translators of the Septuagint, the Greek version of the Old Testament translated during the period of Hellenistic domination, translated *chokmah* with the word *sōtēria*, which is the New Testament term for "salvation." They also sometimes translated *shalom* (the Hebrew word usually translated "peace") with *sōtēria*. Here we see a probable connection of the dominant theme of deliverance to a place of ease and peace.

There is also a note of individual salvation sounded in the apocalyptic vision of the resurrection of the dead. Though originally apparently corporate in character, this idea came to refer to just and unjust individuals, and as such came to exercise a controlling influence in the New Testament.[1]

From the foregoing discussion it will be apparent that the view of salvation in the Old Testament is predominantly this-worldly—a vision of the community of the faithful living in covenant relationship to God, keeping his law. The apocalyptic vision of the end-time is not fundamentally a break with this idea, for the final battle between good and evil takes place on the plane of history, not in a transhistorical, timeless "heaven."[2] Nevertheless, in the idea of resurrection it contained the germ of a "two realm" understanding of soteriology, in which reality, though still in time, would be radically transformed.

The idea of deliverance from external forces received the most modification of any of these elements in the development of a sense of corporate and individual sin. Corporate sin (which involves individual sin) is a major theme of the prophets, and the famous prayer of confession in Ps. 51, for instance, is filled with references to individual sin from which the psalmist seeks deliverance. Nevertheless, the idea of salvation is not usually connected directly to the question of sin, but rather to its consequences. Sin kindles the wrath of God who then sends an agent of destruction to punish Israel. In the apocalyptic visions the element of sin diminishes in importance and the actions of God in history are attributed more to his plan which he works out in accordance with his inscrutable will.[3]

When we turn to the conception of health in the Old Testament, we are struck by its relatively infrequent occurrence. The principal word is *marpe*, which means literally "mended" or "darned." It is found in Proverbs and only once in Jeremiah (ch. 8:15).[4] It is usually applied to the state of wholeness of the individual, in much the same way that we use the term "health" today. Though it has no special relationship to salvation as we have been discussing, nevertheless, like all of life, it is under the reign of God, who may give it or take it away. It is in the same class with flocks, herds, and family—a sign of God's favor.[5] The term *shalom* is sometimes translated "health," as in Ps. 38:3, which suggests that the notions of peace, ease, and health do sometimes overlap.

Another term, *arukah* (literally, "lengthening"), is never used to apply to individuals but only by the prophets to speak of the "health" of the nation, analogically, as in Jer. 8:22:

> Is there no balm in Gilead?
> Is there no physician there?
> Why then has the health of the daughter of my people
> not been restored?

Although this is clearly a case of poetic imagery and not intended literally, its use here and in similar passages linked the idea of health to that of salvation, which has important consequences in the New Testament. The verb form *rapha* ("to heal") is used both literally and figuratively (as in the Servant Song in Isa. 53:5: "And with his stripes we are healed"), which is a further indication of the association of the two ideas that began in the period of the great prophets.

Nevertheless, it is correct to say that throughout the period of the Old Testament salvation and health remained essentially separate ideas, though occasionally linked, especially toward the end of the period. This linkage seems rooted in the Hebrew assumption that the body and the spirit cannot be divorced. There is, of course, no such thing as the salvation of the soul (*nephish*), or even the spirit (*ruach*) in the Old Testament apart from the body. The land of the dead (*Sheol*) is a shadowy place of half life, but not of salvation. This unity of the person made healing and health a choice metaphor for the prophets in speaking of the remedy for the tribulations of the nation of Israel, and led to a striking development to be described in the next section.

2. The New Testament

Salvation is generally accepted as one of the central ideas, if not indeed *the* central idea, of the whole New Testament. Though the noun form *sōtēria* (literally, "soundness," "safety") is not so common as we might think, occurring only forty-three times, the verb form *sōdzō* ("to save") is more common, and both are pervasive in the New Testament literature. This does not indicate, however, that they mean the same thing in all places. Modern scholarship has rather clearly distinguished major theologies in the New Testament which have rather different notions of salvation.

The earliest written materials are generally regarded to be the Pauline corpus (though some of it, notably Ephesians and Colossians, is much later), and it contains the concept of salvation which became controlling in the West. Specifically, salvation refers to the forgiveness of sins of the individual by grace through faith in Christ, and his subsequent reconciliation with God, within the context of the Christian community. Salvation has past, present, and future dimensions, with an impending final consummation seen in a general resurrection and judgment.[6]

In the Johannine literature, salvation is seen primarily as "eternal life" which means both duration and a changed quality of life beginning in the present for those who believe in Jesus. These books are later than the Pauline corpus and reflect a development of the doctrine of salvation as a changed and purified way of life (not absent in Paul, to be sure) while the Final Judgment motif has faded in importance.

The third major theology is that of the Synoptic Gospels, which, though written at a later time than the earliest Pauline material, appear to reflect a very primitive oral tradition in the early church. Since the breakthrough in understanding of this tradition achieved by Albert Schweitzer more than a half century ago scholars have increasingly recognized the

controlling influence of apocalyptic thought patterns, even
when they have not agreed with Schweitzer's thesis that Jesus,
having become disillusioned that the end did not come after
his proclamation of it, deliberately went to the cross to force
the hand of God.[7] Salvation is seen primarily as escape from
the destruction of the chaos to come, and is had by repentance
and faith that Jesus is the true Messiah who comes to warn
men of its coming and to save the righteous. Salvation is not
completely in the future, however, for Jesus sometimes an-
nounces that it has come in the present, as in the case of
Zacchaeus, the publican (Luke 19:9). The link between the
present and the future in this tradition is the clue to understanding the relationship between salvation and health in the
New Testament.

In turning to the theme of healing and health, we can note
first that Paul was apparently little interested in it at all and
mentions it only once.[8] In the Gospel of John, healing is
always a "sign" that the Messiah has come—along with other
miracles. As such it represents a development of the apocalyptic tradition which no longer looks to the future but pro-
claims its arrival in the present.[9]

The situation in the Synoptic Gospels is much more complex.
Here healing is near the heart of the gospel. While it is clear
that it sometimes is a "sign" associated with the end-time, it
is more than this in some places. The verbs meaning "to heal,"
therapeuō ("to serve") and *iaomai* ("to cure"), are common
in the Synoptic Gospels, and twice we find that *sōdzō*, which
as we have seen primarily means "to save" in the New Testament, must be translated "to heal" (Mark 5:23 and Luke 8:36).
Apparently the Synoptic writers made no clear-cut distinctions
among these terms. Further, in one instance *sōdzō* appears
to have been intended to have the double meaning "to save"
and "to heal." This occurs in Mark 5:34 at the close of the account of the woman who was healed of a flow of blood: "And
he said to her, 'Daughter, your faith has made you well
(*sōdzō*); go in peace, and be healed (*hugiēs;* literally, "be

whole") of your disease.'" Healing is frequently said to have resulted from faith, as in this instance, but not invariably, nor is it always associated with the forgiveness of sins.

Viewed from the perspective of apocalyptic, these healings are not humanitarian acts but the initial step in a salvatory process that will be consummated at the end-time, as well as signs that the Messiah has come.[10] Beginning with the prophetic tradition of Isaiah and Jeremiah, as we have noted, healing became by analogy associated with the restoration of the nation. Though not a prominent feature of later apocalyptic, healing was fused into this tradition by Jesus from the prophetic tradition from which he quoted at the beginning of his ministry:

> The spirit of the Lord is upon me
> because he has anointed me
>   to preach good news to the poor.
> He has sent me to proclaim
>   release to the captives
> and recovering of sight to the blind,
> to set at liberty those who are oppressed,
> to proclaim the acceptable year of the Lord.
>   (Luke 4:18.)

This prophecy in The Book of Isaiah (ch. 61:1–2) did not contain the reference to healing in the original, but it is consonant with the theme of the text, which is the restoration and triumph of Israel, described elsewhere as "healing." The apocalyptic tradition with its emphasis on bodily resurrection could readily find a place for healing as a part of the salvatory process, and Jesus appears to have had something of this in mind when he announced that healing was an integral part of his gospel. This is not to say, however, that it was a *necessary* part of it for everyone. It was one element in a cluster of noetic salvatory events associated with the approaching end, in which a kind of "prerealization" of the final salvation beyond the final cataclysmic intervention by God could be glimpsed and experienced, for "those who have ears to hear." [11]

With these matters before us, we are now in a position to assess the relationship between salvation and health in the New Testament in more general fashion. What we have in the Bible is a kind of gradual movement toward convergence, beginning with the prophets and continuing with the postexilic emphasis on the individual; actual, though partial, convergence briefly in the Synoptic accounts; and then another gradual separation as the Parousia (Second Coming of Christ at the end) was delayed, and salvation took on specialized meanings in Paul and John not directly related to health.[12] To be sure, the early church practiced healing as a special gift, along with others, such as teaching and speaking in tongues. Though it is mentioned occasionally, and specific procedures are outlined in James 5:14–15, the urgency and the mood of expectation that pervade the Synoptics is gone. As we shall see, this trend continued in the early church.

In concluding our discussion of salvation and health in the Bible, let us recall the original communal emphasis of the Old Testament, and ask whether this disappeared in the New Testament. Though the individual, rather than the community, is called upon to respond to the message of salvation, the locus of salvation continues to be in the community. Some scholars even suggest that the doctrine of bodily resurrection was understood primarily in terms of transformation rather than the continuing existence of the individual. This transformation was viewed as proof of the faithfulness and the justice of God, but its specific character was not in focus.[13]

Health seems vital to the ability of the individual to participate in the community, even though its importance is not stressed in the later writings of the New Testament. From our modern point of view, therefore, it is tempting to say that health in the New Testament provides for the *possibility* of salvation.[14] Although this idea is not incompatible with the Synoptic picture, the category of possibility is not an important one in the Bible as such, where the march of events is seen as being under the control of God. Health, rather, is one element, when coming as a result of charismatic healing, that signifies that the healed person is participating in the end-time. This is the central point, though healing out of concern for suffering is not absent, especially from the later epistles, as we have noted.

3. The Church to the Reformation

The divergence between salvation and health, which we noted already in progress in the New Testament, continued to grow wider in the early church, though healing was recognized as part of the ministry of the church and as a special gift. After Christianity became the official religion of the Roman Empire it was practiced in more perfunctory fashion through anointing, as the original charismatic power of the gospel, which had sustained it in persecution, continued to ebb.[15]

The theology of the early Middle Ages was dominated by the towering figure of Augustine of Hippo, who completed the fusion of the Pauline emphasis of sin and grace through faith with a Neoplatonic view of man that stressed the imprisonment of the soul in the body. This dualism led to an increasing asceticism in the life of the medieval church, which meant an attitude of indifference or even outright hostility toward the body. The official theology of the church concentrated on getting the soul of the believer into heaven, through the Sacraments, or at least on saving it from hell, as the doctrine of purgatory developed.

In spite of this dualistic understanding of man, however, there developed in the Middle Ages a great interest in healing in the church as the veneration of saints and the belief in the miraculous powers of their relics grew. Initially a kind of para-theology of the church, the lore surrounding relics and their healing properties, began to influence the manuals for pastors compiled by bishops and others responsible for the guidance of the parish priests.[16] The Fourth Lateran Council in 1215, which did so much to codify the beliefs and practices of the medieval church, officially recognized the possible connection between sin and disease, and urged that priests be present to minister to the sick prior to the physician, "so that after spiritual health has been restored to them, the application of bodily medicine may be of greater benefit." [17]

In the middle of the thirteenth century Thomas Aquinas produced his *Summa* of medieval theology, based on the hierarchical understanding of man found in Aristotle rather than Platonic dualism. Here the body and the mind were presented as related and necessary for spiritual development, if not of equal worth. Supernature was viewed as building upon nature rather than subduing it. This completed the process of bringing the body and its needs back into the ambit of salvation, if only peripherally. In Thomas' vision, which was shared by his epoch, nothing was alien to the sphere of God's activity, including health.

Though this continued as the official view of the church until the Reformation (and indeed, in the Roman Catholic Church until the present time, when it is being radically questioned), its relationship to actual practice in the church became clouded by developments signaling the end of the medieval period. The world began to seem more and more an evil place, dominated by the devil and his minions, the witches and demons. In the fourteenth century the black plague decimated the population of Europe, and struck fear into the hearts of those who survived. This fear easily became hysterical when confronted with evils of mysterious origin and beyond man's control.[18] It was easy to assume that they were of supernatural origin, and witch hunts for those who were thought to destroy both the soul and the body became common and remained so until the seventeenth century and the dawn of the Enlightenment.

This meant that, while healing continued as a sacramental practice, it became increasingly associated with exorcism and the struggle with the supernatural powers of darkness. No longer was the world under the rule of God, but of Satan. Individuals sought reconciliation with God, who could save their souls out of the entrapments of the world, as *The Imitation of Christ* amply testifies.[19] If the health of the body was not forgotten, it was once again generally relegated to the status of a matter of relative indifference, which might well be sacrificed to gain eternal bliss. This was the situation that obtained as Martin Luther grew toward manhood at the turn of the sixteenth century.

4. Reformation to the Present

Luther was, of course, the principal innovator in theology after Biblical times. Yet this innovation, radical as it was, did not extend very far beyond his central doctrine of justification by faith alone. In this doctrine he attacked the whole sacramental and sacerdotal system of the medieval church, but not its fundamental assumptions about the world, man, and God. He challenged the means of grace, but not the necessity therefor. Nor did he ever move beyond the late medieval view that the devil is the prince of this world, and Luther's bouts with the devil are celebrated. He did not accept the dualism which rejected the body, but did see it as a realm of Satan's activity. Man lives in Satan's kingdom and in God's at the same time. Hence, Luther was not concerned much about health and its relation to salvation. To save one's soul through faith was enough. "The body they may kill," he wrote, referring to the devils who filled the world. Nevertheless, he did pray for healing on occasion, on grounds of compassion.

John Calvin was even more inclined than Luther to emphasize the salvation of the soul. He viewed medieval healing practices with disdain, ironically mocking the use of relics. Further, he held that the age of miracles was past, including healing by nonphysical means, except by direct divine action. Calvin's more "modern" attitude toward health became a part

of the tradition associated with his name, and it came to be
regarded as essentially unrelated to salvation in a positive
sense. Illness, along with other distressing experiences, was
still often considered to be divine punishment or testing.[20]

From the sixteenth century to the twentieth there was perhaps a greater dichotomy between salvation and health among
Protestants than at any other period in Christian history. Since
this period was discussed from a slightly different angle in the
preceding chapter, I shall not go over the same ground again
in any detail. Suffice it to say that the body-soul distinction
and the compartmentalization of the mind, so that salvation
was presumed to involve primarily only one aspect of it (feeling or willing), meant that the interaction of mind and body
was for the most part disregarded. We have noted the effort
of Jonathan Edwards to overcome some of these problems—
efforts that proved abortive.

At the beginning of the twentieth century two kinds of developments began to alter the attitude of the main line
churches toward the question of health. The first of these was
the rise of Christian Science, which dramatically showed that
religion and healing could be brought together in such fashion
as to attract thousands, however inadequate it might be theo-
logically. Since that time all the main line churches have developed healing movements which continued strongly until
the present time, though sometimes tolerated on the fringes
rather than taken into the heart of the church's life. The
other development was the work of Freud and his successors
in producing a dynamic psychology which plainly showed that
man could not be compartmentalized into body-mind, mind-
spirit categories, or any other categories. Rather, he is one
organic interconnected and interrelated whole which can be
divided into parts that can be discussed and analyzed only as
relatively separable entities.

In recent years a considerable amount of progress has been
made toward understanding the relationship between salvation
and health, and to this we now turn. For after massive resist-

ance over a period of many years, since about 1950, several astute thinkers in the church have been devoting their attention to this question, both directly and indirectly.

NOTES

1. In Ezek., ch. 37, we have the earliest reference to resurrection as a corporate phenomenon, and in Isa., ch. 26, probably the earliest reference to the resurrection of individuals.

2. Bernhard W. Anderson, *Understanding the Old Testament* (Prentice-Hall, Inc., 1957), p. 518.

3. In Dan., ch. 11, we have an example of this in the recital of the rise and fall of empires according to the divine plan.

4. In Jer. 8:15 the term is used poetically to speak of "a time of healing" in the context of a prophecy of doom for the people of Judah. It is not explicitly corporate, even so, and could be understood as referring to the "healing" of individuals. Cf. Jer. 8:22, discussed in the text following.

5. Job is, of course, the great challenge to this understanding of health as a reward for righteousness. The issue is not really resolved either in Job or in the Old Testament as a whole.

6. In Pauline thought the past dimension is clearly the atoning work of Christ on the cross confirmed by his resurrection, and the present is the appropriation of this through faith. The future dimension is not so clear, however. For, alongside the idea of general bodily resurrection is the idea of immediate entry into heaven at death (Phil. 1:23). These ideas occur without resolution in Paul, and persist in the eschatology of the church to the present time. The notion of a disembodied soul is foreign to Paul, though later connected to his idea of immediate fellowship with Christ at death. The emphasis is on general resurrection as vindication of God's promise to redeem creation, including the body.

7. Albert Schweitzer, *The Quest of the Historical Jesus,* 3d ed. (London: A. & C. Black, Ltd., 1954).

8. In I Cor., ch. 12, as a spiritual gift. In Acts 28:8, Paul is said to have performed a healing, further evidence that he regarded

it as a legitimate function, even if not specially related to salvation.

9. The phrase "realized eschatology" has been used by modern scholars, following C. H. Dodd, to designate this emphasis.

10. The idea of salvatory process is admittedly not a Biblical notion as such. Nevertheless, this phrase seems appropriate to designate the New Testament view of salvation occurring as a chain of events with links integrally related. Cf. the idea of prolepsis developed by Wolfhart Pannenberg, "The Revelation of God in Jesus of Nazareth," in James M. Robinson and John B. Cobb, Jr. (eds.), *Theology as History*, Vol. III of New Frontiers in Theology (Harper & Row, Publishers, Inc., 1967), pp. 112–113, *et passim*, in which present events are viewed as participating in future events which give them their meaning.

11. The authenticity of Jesus' healing ministry is not an issue here, nor the compassion for suffering which characterized his healing. Much evidence suggests that both of these were dimensions of his brief history. Nevertheless, they were not the central issues for him or his contemporaries, as they are likely to be for us today.

12. This process, which might be called the "spiritualization" of salvation in the later New Testament, may have been due in large measure to the problem that the New Testament writers faced in the Gnostic ideas present in their culture. Gnosticism stressed the radical dualism of the soul and the body, matter and spirit. Though the New Testament writers never adopted these ideas, they did apparently write so that they could be understood by those familiar with them.

13. Leander E. Keck, "New Testament Views of Death," in Liston O. Mills (ed.), *Perspectives on Death* (Abingdon Press, 1969), pp. 97–98. Keck does not deny that the resurrection of the person is a New Testament idea, but says, "The central issue is not whether man has an essence that survives, but whether the God in whom he believes, however falteringly, has enough moral integrity to 'make good' with the life he himself called into existence."

14. Vincent Eareckson, "*Sodzo* and Cognates in the New Testament" (unpublished paper, Princeton Theological Seminary, 1969), p. 19. Eareckson does not say that this was the view of

the New Testament, but that from our point of view "it would be fair to say that Jesus, when he healed a person, opened up for him the *possibility* of life and salvation, not the assurance of it."

15. William A. Clebsch and Charles R. Jaekle, *Pastoral Care in Historical Perspective* (Prentice-Hall, Inc., 1964), p. 20.

16. *Ibid.*, p. 24.

17. *Ibid.*, p. 25.

18. Johan Huizinga, *The Waning of the Middle Ages* (London: E. Arnold and Co., 1924), p. 21.

19. Thomas à Kempis, *The Imitation of Christ,* tr. by Abbot Justin McCann (Mentor Press, 1957).

20. John Calvin, *Institutes of the Christian Religion,* tr. by Henry Beveridge, 2 vols. (London: James Clarke & Company, Ltd., 1953), Vol. II, p. 196. Calvin emphasized strongly praying only within the bounds set by the Lord's Prayer, which makes no mention of healing as such (*ibid.*, p. 198).

Chapter III

The Contemporary Situation

1. Some Principal Attempts at Understanding the Relationship

The decade of the 1950's saw several able persons turn their attention to the question of how therapeutic and salvatory processes are related. Most of them took a position which, in spite of some significant differences among them, could be called *inclusionist*. Chief among these was David E. Roberts, whose careful discussion of the implications of psychotherapy for traditional Protestant understandings of salvation set the mood for the discussion to follow. Roberts concluded, after his sympathetic though penetrating analysis of the issues, that salvation includes healing and that any attempt to keep them separate is bound to fail.[1] He did not elaborate on this conclusion to any great extent, but in this statement provided the basis for the development of the inclusionist position that salvation includes healing, whatever else it may include.

Others following in this discussion were anxious to convey this central point. Josef Goldbrunner on the Catholic side made a virtual equation of salvation and health (understood in Jungian terms) in his book *Holiness Is Wholeness*.[2] Seward Hiltner in his *Preface to Pastoral Theology* presented healing as a subperspective of shepherding, and discussed it as a dominant theme in the book.[3] Even Albert C. Outler, who took a very wary attitude toward psychotherapy as being involved with a materialistic, godless, philosophical outlook, nevertheless affirmed that the church needs the practical wisdom that psychotherapy can offer.[4] The decade closed with a major Protestant denomination, The United Presbyterian Church U.S.A., officially affirming the inclusionist position in its pamphlet *The Relationship of the Christian Faith to Health*.[5]

To be sure, these and other writers were aware of some of the ambiguities in the problem, and were often dialectically sophisticated in treating them, but, with the significant exception of Eduard Thurneysen, they all viewed health and healing to be directly involved in the salvatory process.[6]

Thus, by the beginning of the decade of the 1960's the long separation of salvation and health had been finally overcome, at least among many leaders in the churches, and had begun to be overcome at the grass-roots level. Since that time interest in the problem has continued unabated, but the focus of this interest has shifted from *whether* and *to what extent* the salvation and health processes are related, to *how* they are related. The relationship has come to be assumed to be a substantial one, but the question of methods of relating salvation and health had become uppermost as the basic clue to understanding contemporary life in the church. Hence we may call the '60s the era of *dialectical clarification* of the problems and possibilities in relating salvation and health.

The first of these writers was Daniel Day Williams, who, from his viewpoint in constructive or systematic theology, published *The Minister and the Care of Souls* in 1961.[7] He saw the connection between salvation and health in what he termed the principle of linkage, by which he meant that all of man's life is related to all its parts—hence nothing is foreign either to salvation or to health.[8] In particular cases, he held, it is not possible to define *in advance* what the relationship may be, though in retrospect the lines of relationship may be discerned.[9] He did make one rather categorical distinction, saying that "the measure of man's life is not his freedom from inner struggle, but his discovery of how the whole of life, including its dark side, can be brought into the service of growth in love. In this sense salvation must transcend all particular therapies." [10]

This quotation gives an important clue to Williams' whole outlook, and elsewhere in his book we find him stressing the church as a healing and saving community. He does not, however, spell out the distinction he has drawn, and his principle of interpenetrating linkage really goes against such spelling out.[11]

Next, Edward E. Thornton in his *Theology and Pastoral Counseling* showed one way in which it could be spelled out.[12] Thornton described salvation as the sphere of ultimate concern and health as the *penultimate,* that is, the next to the last stage.[13] Thornton showed clearly that either psychotherapy or pastoral counseling might be successfully used to assist a person toward health, and suggested that this in turn would prepare him for encounter with God, the ultimate. In doing this, he further pointed out that "salvation is potential in health," just as health is potential in salvation.[14]

Thornton thus proposed that the health-salvation relationship is similar to a two-stage rocket, in which the first stage must be fired before getting to the second. This model has considerable merit, for it clearly shows salvation's dependence upon health. But it has the disadvantage of an "all or nothing at all" model. Unless one attains a certain optimal level of health, presumably he could never "encounter" God at all. Thus, although in some respects he made an advance beyond Williams in clarifying the relationship, in a crucial matter we seem to be better off with the relative fuzziness of Williams' position, which has the advantage of allowing persons to participate in salvation without a particular kind of therapeutic experience.

In 1966, Thomas C. Oden joined the contributors to this discussion with his *Kerygma and Counseling,* and followed it a year later with *Contemporary Theology and Psychotherapy.*[15]

Although his position is considerably developed and expanded in the second volume, for our purposes they may be treated together. Oden is concerned to reconcile his understanding of psychotherapy—primarily the model developed by Carl R. Rogers and his colleagues—with a Barthian view of theology. Holding that most scholars in this field have used a "natural theology" model in which they moved from man and the world to God as a fundamental methodological assumption, he proposed to reverse this assumption and move from God to man via an analogy of faith which finds the true state of affairs in revelation and then can identify similar modes and relationships in the world. Thus he finds in Rogerian psychotherapy analogies to the themes of divine self-disclosure and self-giving love, and in the world evidence for the "cosmic Christ." [16]

Elsewhere I have discussed the merits of this position in some detail.[17] Here we need only note that Oden, in effect, views psychotherapy as a fragmentary, though apparently real (based on what he calls an ontology of acceptance) version of salvation. It is not really "included" in salvation as revealed in the Word of God, but is rather a secular manifestation of the same processes viewed as an aspect of creation.[18] He has shown more explicitly than others the parallels between some Biblical motifs and some psychotherapeutic motifs (though he was not the first, by any means, to point them out). Healing done by ministers or laymen through pastoral counseling inside the church presumably would be regarded in the same way as psychotherapy, that is, as ambiguous and partial but genuine salvation.[19]

At about the same time as Oden's work appeared, Don S. Browning published his *Atonement and Psychotherapy*, like Oden's work an exploration of Rogerian psychotherapy and aspects of theology.[20] But instead of revelation, Browning concentrates on the doctrine of the atonement, using a two-way analogical approach which permits him to draw insights from psychotherapy to illumine the atonement, as well as the other way around. Browning does enrich our understanding of atone-

ment through this approach, especially our understanding of
Irenaeus' *Christus Victor* theory, which stresses the bondage
of man to the powers of darkness and his liberation by Christ's
defeat of the devil. Like Oden, Browning sees in psychotherapy
an ontology of acceptance and a kind of revelation, but unlike
Oden, he does not have to distinguish between partial and full
salvation, and apparently sees healing and salvation as ways
of understanding the same kinds of processes. He does give us
another dimension to both in his drawing an analogy between
the suffering of the therapist and the suffering of the self-
giving God.

Although Browning has gone farther than anyone in dis-
closing the analogies and even putative identities of aspects
of healing and of salvation, by this very disclosure he has apparently torn down some of the distinctions that we have
found being made. If psychotherapy and atonement, rightly
understood, are this similar, how can one say that the one is
partial, penultimate, or is "transcended" by the other? Have
we not in fact found in Browning that all real distinction between healing and salvation *as we have come to understand
it in the liberal Protestant tradition* disappears? Could it be
that our notion of salvation is really a very limited one, con-
fined essentially to the individual as the locus and beneficiary
of salvation? Although the writers whom we have discussed
are all very much concerned about social issues, they do not
really connect their treatment of the health-salvation relationship to social concerns, except in a global way. Nor do they
deal with the problem posed by death—the end of all healing
as we know it—which faces every man. Their model is essentially the psychotherapeutic one, despite methodological
differences. They see in the therapeutic process something
valuable, but beyond it they tend to become formalistic and
abstract. I believe they went as far as they could, given the
models of health and salvation with which they were working,
largely developed before 1950.[21] Hence, valuable as their contributions have been, we must look beyond them with the

help of developments taking place independently in theology and the health sciences while they were working. To these we now turn.[22]

2. Salvation in Contemporary Theology

In the post "God is dead" situation of contemporary theology two approaches toward understanding the God-man relationship have appeared which have genuine promise—process theology and the theology of history. Actually, they appeared before the "God is dead" phenomenon, but could not get the hearing they deserved until the antirational movement in theology which had dominated it for so long came to an end with the death of "God." Of the two, process theology has been far more significant in the development of my own thinking, so I shall turn first to it.

The central figure in the development of process philosophy, which lies behind process theology, was Alfred North Whitehead. For the first part of his career a mathematician, Whitehead gradually turned to philosophy in middle life. His background in mathematics gave him an extraordinary grasp of the logic of events, but it also contributed to giving him a writing style which is hard to penetrate in his principal theoretical works. Nevertheless, we must get some of his key ideas before us in order to understand what a vision of salvation in process theology looks like.[23]

Whitehead called his philosophy the philosophy of organism, by which he focused attention on the relatedness of all events and their purposive development through time. He held that the notion of "substance" is one of the fundamental errors of Western thinking, for in reality "substances" are relatively enduring processes made up of events or occasions. Substance, then, is the primary example of what Whitehead called "the fallacy of misplaced concreteness," that is, the idea that we are dealing with fundamental reality when we apprehend something relatively solid, resistive, and "material." Nor are ideas the really real. Rather, reality is composed of "actual occasions" having a mental and a physical pole.

The elements that must come together to form such dipolar occasions are (a) creativity, or the primal energy of the universe, (b) the eternal objects, or the abstract possibilities existing in the universe, and (c) God—the principle of limitation or concreteness, who "envisages" the values accruing from the ingression of the eternal objects into actual occasions or events, contributing to the event an important aspect of its "subjective aim" or purpose.[24] Although such actual occasions are microcosmic and almost instantaneous, each does have a "life" in which it develops toward the "satisfaction" of its aim.

Whitehead understood all of reality (with the exception of God, who has some, but not all, the characteristics of an actual occasion) to be made up of such occasions, which form hierarchies of events in the space-time continuum called "nexus" and "societies." Animals are highly complex societies of occasions, and human beings the most complex and differentiated societies. Like all other occasions, nexuses, and societies, they attempt to realize the "satisfaction" of their subjective aim, but through the phenomenon of consciousness, and the relative freedom accompanying it, they gain a part in the determination of that aim not shared by any except perhaps the most advanced "societies," although a degree of freedom is technically inherent in every occasion.

Occasions are related to one another and to eternal objects through what Whitehead calls "prehensions," or feelings. Though feeling in the ordinary language sense is included in this term, it means much more than that. It includes all the relationships of temporal sequence, cause and effect, found in the "physical pole" of occasions, and all the experiences of thought, awareness, perception, and affect found in the "mental pole" of occasions. Through this mental pole, all occasions are at least potentially related to all other occasions, as well as to the eternal objects (through "conceptual prehensions"), since telepathy has established that physical contiguity is not necessary for communication. In the doctrine of prehension Whitehead took account of the richness, complexity, and depth of experience, and also overcame the traditional view of the subject-object dichotomy of Western thought by showing the participation of events in the experience of other events, all of which are both subjects and objects. The universe was no longer seen as a vast billiard table upon which objects collided but did not relate intrinsically.

Whitehead understood value primarily in aesthetic terms, and hence held that the subjective aim of all occasions is ultimately toward beauty, a certain harmony of proportions and relations. The thwarting of this aim toward beauty by other occasions is how he understood evil—the mutually obstructive character of things.[25] These two elements, beauty and evil, constitute the core concepts in Whitehead's understanding of ethics and morality, and to them traditional problems of responsibility, love, and justice are related. The overall picture is that of the creative advance into novelty and increased value, though evil as tragedy constantly prevents the satisfaction of many subjective aims.

Even at best, however, beauty fades and perishes. "Time is a perpetual perishing." [26] Whitehead came to hold that this final problem is overcome by these values being preserved in the life of God himself. This aspect of God's nature he called the consequent nature of God, by which he meant God's actualizing and developing of himself through the occasions of the world. God as the principle of limitation, which we noted earlier, he called the primordial nature of God, an abstraction from his actual, consequent nature. Unlike actual occasions, which perish, God continues to actualize himself throughout eternity. He is "everlasting." [27]

In the light of this albeit brief, simplified treatment of Whitehead's outlook, I think we can nonetheless see its meaning for the doctrine of salvation. Salvation, in this view, *must refer primarily to the preservation in the life of God of the values realized in the world, especially in the lives of men.*

Although personal survival after death cannot be ruled out, at least for a time,[28] what is saved is not the entity of the person, whether conceived in bodily or purely "spiritual" terms, but rather his *personhood*, that is, the qualities that form the gestalt of his person, and represent the contribution that he made to the stream of life. These qualities are preserved as active dimensions of the life of God, contributing to his development, not as a frozen monument. While it is true that values can also be preserved in relatively "frozen" form in works of art, political constitutions, and social conventions and traditions, they are constantly being modified and some are lost altogether by the inroads of evil. Or they may be fused in creative emergent events into new shapes which make them scarcely recognizable.

From the point of view of process theology, to use now the narrower term, Jesus Christ is such an emergent, in fact, the supreme creative emergent. Through ministry, death, and "resurrection" he set in motion the power toward love and hope which characterized primitive Christianity and which subsequently infused Western culture. Though this power has never been unambiguously expressed either inside or outside the church, it still continues to manifest itself in the self-giving idealism of many individuals and even institutions, however ambiguous. This is not an "exemplary" theory of the atonement, but as Browning has pointed out, has more in common with the *Christus Victor* view of the early church.[29]

Looking back to the New Testament view of salvation, we can, I think, see some striking parallels. Salvation is participation in divine events, not an isolated experience of relief from guilt. It is both corporate and individual, with the individual finding his salvation in the life of God, but only on the basis of actualization of his personhood. The individual comes to participate in it by linking himself to the stream of history in which the salvatory process is manifested, and by responding to the "lure" of God's call into a future with him.

The major problem with process theology, as a theology that

can lead to action, is its lack of what might be called an "urgency" principle. One may well concede that ultimately one's personal values will be preserved in the life of God, and still be relatively unaffected in one's daily life. It doesn't "grab" one to know that God's everlastingness and sympathy will somehow "make up" for the suffering of the present, however reassuring it might be intellectually. The element of crisis, of impending decisive events, is missing.

In developing his theology of history, Wolfhart Pannenberg is beginning to provide this missing element. While his position is quite compatible with Whitehead's in most respects, his concern is to find the empirical, historical basis of the New Testament theology and its consequences in subsequent Western, and even world, history.[30] He finds the atmosphere of expectation generated by the apocalyptic milieu decisive, and its fulfillment in the resurrection event the key to the New Testament. Far from dismissing the resurrection as a wish fulfillment, as modern theology has generally tended to do (when it has not treated it as myth), he seeks to understand what the actual event may have been. This is so because Pannenberg understood the resurrection as the "proleptic" dawning of the reign of God [31]—that is, an event participating internally in the future Kingdom of God.

He does not understand this event as literally resuscitation, however, but regards "resurrection" as a metaphor from the apocalyptic tradition which the disciples of Jesus used to "describe the indescribable." [32] As such it is not an isolated event, but "the end of a process of unveiling." [33]

It is the anticipation of the culmination of the Kingdom that gives Pannenberg's theology its "futuristic" cast, and leads to its frequent association with the position of the "theology of hope" of Jürgen Moltmann. But actually they differ significantly in method and outlook, since Moltmann's stance is basically in the dialectical tradition of Barth, and Pannenberg is a radical empiricist, seeking to find revelation in the events of history. Both do emphasize the "surprise" element in God's future for man, but the discontinuity is more apparent than real in Pannenberg's view, since the meaning of the past can be determined, once the event has occurred, and its "prolepsis" discerned.[34]

When this principle of prolepsis is applied to process theology, a shift in its orientation takes place. Salvation is no longer a process taking place in the present and stretching vaguely into the future, but rather it moves toward a climax that will in turn reveal more fully the meaning of the present. The analogy which is meaningful to me is that of pregnancy and childbirth. The salvatory process is *pregnant,* and we anticipate the outcome without knowing precisely what it will be. There is an element of genuine surprise, no matter how imaginative the expectant family may be! I shall return to this important point in Chapter V, as there are signs that the pregnancy of our particular epoch of the salvatory process may be approaching full term.[35]

Now we must look briefly at how this view of salvation compares with our traditional one. The basic difference, of course, is that it places emphasis on the salvation of personhood rather than on personal entities. Though this personhood is partially saved through its influence (not a metaphor in process terms, but an actual occurrence) on those who come after the person, it is mainly and finally saved through its preservation in and contribution to the life of God. We noted earlier that the salvation of individual entities does not appear to some modern scholars to have been a central concern of the New Testament understanding of resurrection, and the corporate emphasis of the Old Testament is, in any case, not entirely lost. It is our Western tradition which has come to emphasize the individual motifs in the New Testament out of proportion to their original import. Nevertheless, we must not so de-emphasize individual salvation as to have it swallowed up completely in some cosmic beehive. In holding an idea of the salvation of personhood, I am reaffirming what seems to me to be central in the New Testament view.

In the view being set forth here, salvation is from the perishing of time and from evil as mutual destructiveness. This is in contrast to the traditional view of salvation as escape from the punishment due to sin, but more congruent with the Biblical view of salvation as deliverance from external foes and the consequences of sin. In the process view, evil includes sin, as the failure of persons and societies (in the ordinary sense of that term) to fulfill their initial aims, or to fulfill them only partially. Such failure always brings destructive consequences on both those failing and all the occasions to which they are related (our current pollution crisis is an excellent, though terrible, example). Although God is a participant in each occasion, contributing to its subjective aim along with the past and the occasion itself, his contribution is only decisive when that aim is essentially fulfilled. Not all sin is conscious or committed with a full view of the consequences, but it all involves the person's use of his freedom to deflect himself from a full realization of his possibilities.

The idea of salvation from the ravages of time resonates with the Fourth Gospel and the Wisdom Literature.

We may ask, however: What happens to development that is thwarted, to lives cut off before they come to fufillment, to beauty that never has an opportunity to bloom? The answer must be that those values in the occasions of the organism that have been actualized will be preserved, but it is a tragic fact that those cut off are truly gone and can never be actualized in just the way they might have been, though those occasions coming after them may approximate their realization. Each person is unique, and each occasion of his life has its unique features which can never be completely replicated. Thus in this view of salvation both joy and tragedy are coinherent—in some epochs the latter undoubtedly outweighing the former.

Salvation means a progressive response to the lure of God toward the realization of beauty, and the peace which is the preservation of beauty. Thus in the view of salvation presented here, aesthetics rather than purity is the key, as in traditional ideas of sanctification. Though many qualifications have been introduced over the centuries to the basic notion of purity, as it is found, for instance, in Rom., ch. 12, still it dominates discussions of sanctification almost to the present day. Only recently has the idea of development come to displace it, and to date, it tends to be vague at those points most relevant to the question of salvation.[36] Beauty may strike us at first as being too pale and effete an understanding of the goal of the process of sanctification, the history of which is strewn with the bones of martyrs. Understood in depth, however, and not narrowly as something that the individual is cultivating for himself, but rather is seeking for the experience of all that he is related to, it is a truly powerful concept which can lead us to grasp the meaning of religion for our time.[37]

Peace comes finally through the understanding of the preservation of all value in the life of God.[38] But more particularly, it comes through a sense that God does indeed participate in our common life, including its darkness and suffering as well as its joy and light. In Whitehead's language, "He is the great companion—the fellow sufferer who understands." [39] Thus we come a full circle back to the Old Testament conception of salvation as deliverance from distress to a place of ease and peace (*shalom*). Ours is a religious tradition of history, pilgrimage, and crossing the river, but finally there must be the riverbank and the shade of the trees.

Even beyond this there is still more, for the values thus taken into the life of God are poured back into the world through his continual envisagement of possibilities and participation in their actualization in the world. Thus we find that God and world are in constant reciprocal interaction, but without either losing identity to the other. This is not a pantheism, but at most a *panentheism* (God and the world interpenetrating), as Charles Hartshorne has said.[40]

In concluding this section, I note that little or nothing has been said about traditional concepts of guilt, faith, forgiveness, and reconciliation. These will be dealt with in Chapter V, as implications of my total position regarding anthropology are spelled out.

3. Contemporary Conceptions of Health

Modern understandings of health as including what has come to be called "mental" as well as physical dimensions date from the nineteenth century. By the fourth decade of that century, which marked the founding of the American Psychiatric Association, physicians had come to assume responsibility for the care and treatment of bizarre, disturbed, and often bothersome persons, who were then called mentally ill. Of course, terms such as "insanity" have persisted in courts of law, and "craziness" and "madness" in ordinary language to refer to such persons. But in the culture as a whole, illness was increasingly used as the basic category that applied, and by the beginning of the twentieth century the institutions where such persons were kept came generally to be called hospitals, rather than insane asylums.

We need to understand this change as a historical development related much more to the development of the scientific world view and the decline in supernaturalism (in which personal disturbances were often attributed to the powers of darkness) than to any concrete discoveries about the nature of such disturbances. That is, there was no breakthrough in the understanding of "mental illness" as there was in the terrible epidemic diseases caused by bacteria. This must be kept in mind for the discussion that is to follow, in which the nature of illness and health, especially the "mental" aspects of these, will be seen to be far from commanding a consensus.

A further development must be noted before getting into a discussion of the contemporary situation. Subsequent to the work of Freud and the spread of dynamic understanding of personality functioning, many kinds of behaviors such as stealing, lying, loafing, promiscuity, and even felonious as-

sault came to be regarded by professionals in the mental
health field as due to mental illness rather than willful per-
versity. In this way health began to take the place of goodness
as a moral value. However much behavior of the types mentioned above might be deplored, persons who acted in such
ways came to be thought of not as wicked but as ill. This
trend continued to develop through the 1950's, when mental
health assumed the stature of the central goal of human moral
effort for many, if not most, middle- and upper-class people
in our culture. At the same time, increasing doubts about the
nature of mental health were being expressed, and it was
found to defy precise definition.[41] These doubts grew into full-
fledged contradictory positions in the 1960's, which together
with the increasing recognition that alterations in the social
structure, as well as in individuals, are needed to alleviate the
ills of our society have led to a decline in the prestige of
health as a moral value. Yet its importance as a central "value"
category cannot be ignored, and its relationship to other values must be understood if we are to get any real light on the
basic question of anthropology with which we started. To an
analysis of the nature of health, then, we now turn.

We must get before us the main alternative views of health
in order to see clearly the issues involved.

a. *Health as the absence of impairment of structure and
function.* Although this view is held by an assortment of clini-
cians who are not concerned about the theory of health beyond
the need to treat persons who appear with complaints, it is
held theoretically by a sizable group of psychiatrists and psychologists who stress the organic base of functioning. They
insist that the notion of "functional" illness is a fiction, and
that for every functional impairment there must be a structural lesion or chemical disturbance. Though this view is
more commonly held with regard to schizophrenia, where there
is definite evidence of a hereditary factor, it is applied to all
forms of mental and emotional distress by many, who stress
the fact that science has progressed by the discovery of phys-

ical causes for presumed nonphysical difficulties, such as demon possession. Proponents of this view acknowledge that they do not have evidence for the organic basis of many kinds of distress and aberrant behavior, but they insist that this will come. Meanwhile, they attack the functional views, especially psychodynamic ones, stressing the relatively low rate of "cure" by therapeutic modalities based on such positions, a question to which we shall presently return.[42]

Whatever the ultimate theoretical merits of this position, it has some serious defects as an operational definition of health. Apart from its clinical limitations,[43] it depends upon the presence of some salient symptom or behavior to signal the absence of health, which is interpreted by the person (or someone associated with him) as an impairment of function. This can easily be done in some instances, such as appendicitis or acute depression, but not in others, such as mild chronic fatigue or anger expressed through verbal assault. Though such phenomena present some problems for any view of health, they are not even touched by this one unless they come to the attention of a clinician for "treatment." That is, there is a range of behavior and emotional states that are impairments only if one has in mind some *norm* of functioning which goes beyond commonsense notions. These can only be dealt with on an *ad hoc* clinical basis if they are presented for treatment. Then an *implicit* norm of what is proper functioning comes into play, but it is not made explicit, for there is no positive concept of health, only a negative one. For our purposes, we need to know what kinds of ideal health states are thought to be in operation in any approach. In the structure/function impairment view, we do not find this.

b. *Health as coping with internal and external stress.* This was basically the view of Freud, who held that coping was being successfully carried out if a person could love and work. It has recently formed the basis of an important book on health in the Freudian tradition, *The Vital Balance*, by Karl A. Menninger, Paul W. Pruyser, and Martin Mayman.[44] This work also incorporated many developments in psychoanalytic ego psychology, and the position taken is thus close to the one to be presented in this book. Essentially, ego psychology refers to the increased emphasis placed on the ego (as distinguished from the id and the superego) in contemporary psychoanalysis. Though Freud recognized the role of ego increasingly toward the end of his career, his position remained essentially a theory of conflict between the instinctual drives of the id and the demands of society incorporated into the superego, with the ego struggling to mediate and mitigate the conflict through contact with reality. In ego psychology this role is retained, but the ego is conceived of as having a "conflict free" sphere of its own, and of having increased control over the total life of the person, so that it has come to be regarded as the "executive" of the personality.[45] Its functions include perception and communication, the person's relational tools.

The coping theory as presented by Menninger *et al.* has much to commend it. By taking into account the inner and outer conditions with which the individual must cope, it is able to be specific about health in a way that the impairment theory is not. A series of levels of illness, or "orders of dysfunction" in which the person is viewed as able to cope progressively less and less well when measured by the degree of regression involved and the cost to him and those about him, is presented. The ideal health state is conceived of as being one in which there is little or no regression and the cost of maintaining homeostasis or "the vital balance" of interacting processes is minimal.

The concept of homeostasis (literally, "standing the same"), as developed by Walter Cannon and others, means that by a complicated set of feedback regulatory mechanisms and interaction with the environment an organism maintains itself relatively "the same," even though it is constantly exchanging energy with the environment. Menninger applied this idea developed by Cannon to explain the physical stability of the organism through time, along with the similar idea of "heterostasis," to the mental and emotional life of man. He does show convincingly that this principle is an important one to take into account in understanding health.[46] What often appears to be a bizarre aberration in behavior is in fact an attempt to cope with some form of stress which threatens to upset the vital balance altogether, and often it succeeds, though at great cost.[47] Such aberrations are the person's attempt to maintain his identity, integrity, and sense of worth in the face of what he regards, consciously or unconsciously, as a grave threat to them, and therefore, to his very existence. The behavior *compensates* him for felt losses in these areas, or for anticipated losses, thus maintaining the balance. In the next chapter I shall be discussing this principle of compensation in some detail.

As strong as this position is, however, it leaves one dimension of the human situation almost out of account. This is the factor of development, or forward movement toward greater differentiation and integration of structure and function. Although development is clearly recognized as a prime factor in the young, it is equally important in those who have reached physical maturity. Not only are specific skills sometimes developed by adults, but their personalities as a whole may continue to develop virtually throughout life. If we take coping as the central principle of our understanding of health, we see only the need to maintain balance by returning to a "steady state." Development can only be understood as a form of compensation. That is, one develops new functions in order to compensate for threatened or actual loss.[48] This certainly does occur, and we shall take a close look at it in the next chapter. But development has a quality of freedom and autonomy about it that cannot be finally all subsumed under the idea of compensation. This is clear in a toddler learning to walk, and I hope to make it equally clear in some kinds of adult behavior.

c. *The "blossom" theory of health.* Here we find the developmental principle at the center of the approach to an understanding of health. The basic idea is that if the human personality receives enough nutrients from the environment, both human and nonhuman, it will "blossom," or grow and develop, according to an inner map, or *entelechy*, as Aristotle put it. No inner impediments to this development are presupposed, unless they themselves develop as *compensation* for the lack of adequate environmental nutrients. These nutrients include all the elements necessary for physical and mental development, food, life space, love, intellectual stimulation, companionship, structure.

Among the prominent blossom theorists perhaps Carl R. Rogers, Abraham Maslow, and Erich Fromm are the best known, though Karen Horney, in my judgment, has a more complete and sophisticated understanding of personality dynamics.[49] All these theorists may be called "self-actualization" or "self-realization" theorists. These are terms they use themselves to refer to their positions, and they both point to the core of the personality as they conceive it—the "self" which is to be actualized.[50] I have called them "blossom" theorists in order to emphasize the principle of inner potential being actualized, and the freedom from internal contradiction of this potential which is to be fulfilled. To be sure, these theorists are all realistic enough to see that there are internal conflicts and contradictions, but they contend these conflicts could have been avoided if the environment had been properly nutritive.

One is quickly drawn to the obvious advantages of this position, for it takes into account the core factor in the subjective experience of every human being—the need for freedom to become what he can, or as it is usually put, to be himself. Further, it shows his link to the rest of nature, where the principle of development out of inner programming is everywhere found. And finally, it sets in bold relief the role of the environment in man's existence at a time when we are just discovering the complexities of his interaction with that environment in controversies as different as school busing and the question of phosphates in detergents.

These must be regarded as important considerations in an

adequate view of health. Yet the blossom theory does not really take into sufficient account man's differences from the rest of nature, in two respects. First, his evolution has produced a degree of tension between his "higher" functioning and his "lower" unknown in the rest of nature. Without subscribing to a platonic dualism, we can see this clearly, for instance, in the leaps, starts, and pains of development in early adolescence. In those tribal cultures where this is not so evident, other forms of conflict, often ritualized, obtain.[51] This means that there may well be incompatibility between aspects of the personality which are to be actualized, with the result that some predominate or suppress others. There may be more potential than can possibly be actualized in a lifetime. Moreover, as I have argued elsewhere, the term "self" is misleading in this context. Persons may become actualized, at least in part, but "self" refers to the person's sense of identity and sameness through time. It is essentially a conservator of the past, which, when projected into the future, tends to repeat the past, rather than build novelty upon it.[52]

The second way in which the blossom theory fails to take account of man's distinctiveness from the rest of nature is its tendency to negate the factor of freedom which man has. Though emphasizing the necessity of man's becoming free from the environment, these theorists (with the exception of Jung, if he is included; cf. n. 50) do not take sufficient account of the factor of choice, which enables man to opt for some patterns of interaction and reject others. Without insisting that man is "free" in an absolute philosophical sense (as noted earlier in this chapter, I hold that man has a relative freedom), I do affirm his capacity to choose within limits how he shall behave, and hence what aspects of his personhood will be actualized. For without developing patterns of behavior, there is no actualization of potential—whether we are discussing becoming a skilled baseball player or practitioner of the *koan* meditation. Often, through this process of choice, potentials are irrevocably lost and can never be realized. Hence there is a tragic note in the process of human development which is not present in the blossom theory. Without this recognition a conception of health inevitably tends toward a romanticism in which contact with reality is lost, and despair sets in.

d. *Mental health as an illusion: extreme cultural views.* Theorists who hold this view agree with position "a" that health is essentially a matter of structural/functional impairment. But they limit this view to physical health, holding that what is normally referred to as mental illness is due to problems of communication or to a lack of social role identity. Thomas Szasz and Theodore R. Sarbin are two contemporary exponents of this position.[53] Though differing in some respects, they agree that mental health and mental illness are a "myth" or at best metaphors which point to disturbances that actually have no organic base (except in clearly neurological conditions). These disturbances are real enough, but, contend these theorists, their association with notions of illness is due to historical accidents rather than to any intrinsic relationship, and is perpetuated by the medical profession, who have a vested interest in it.

We have noted that there is at least some historical basis for their contention that mental illness and health are not intrinsically related to physical illness and health. Moreover, there undoubtedly are important social and cultural factors involved. Patterns of mental illness do vary from culture to culture.[54] Also, critics such as Sarbin and Szasz have done everyone a service by calling sharp attention to the inadequacies of present concepts of mental illness and treatment, resulting in social stigmas for those afflicted with it—especially the more severe forms which are likely to be labeled schizophrenic—tantamount to calling a person a hopeless menace.

Nevertheless, there are some elements in these disturbances which do seem like illness—their often sudden onset and remission, for instance, suggesting an analogy to a fever. Further, some forms of mental illness do seem to have a hereditary base, though it is not clear that this is a sufficient explanation.

The whole concept of "psychosomatic" illness, in which a close relationship between emotional states and physical symptoms has now been rather clearly documented, also presents problems for the extreme cultural view.[55]

4. Toward a Resolution of the Health Question

While it is evident that none of the foregoing positions are adequate in every respect, each contains an important emphasis for any construction of a theory of health. The idea of health as the absence of impairment forces us to take into account the concrete and specific factors involved in speaking of health or the lack of it. Health cannot only be a description of some ideal state rarely or never seen, but must be relevant to actual conditions. The coping theory compels us to take into account the dynamics of resistance to stress in all its modes. The blossom, or fulfillment, model makes us aware of the dimension of developmental potential and striving which characterizes man, without which he would be less than fully human. And, finally, the cultural model of mental health clearly points to its radical relational character, even though it divorces mental health from physical health. All of these must be a part of the concept of health to be developed.

At the present time, thinking about health is tending to be polarized between rather extreme organic (impairment) views on the one side, and equally extreme cultural views on the other. Views based upon personality dynamics have been forced into the background by a variety of factors. Chief among them is the current emphasis on the social aspects of mental health problems, as found in the new Comprehensive Community Mental Health Centers, some progress in understanding chemical aspects of schizophrenia, and the failure of dynamically oriented psychotherapies to be a panacea for all emotional disturbances, which has called into question the personality theory upon which it rests.

Since the view to be presented here is based in part on such a dynamic understanding, I think that something needs to be said in defense of this choice.

Hans Eysenck began an attack upon the effectiveness of psychotherapy in the early 1950's which he and a number of like-minded psychologists and a few psychiatrists have continued until the present time.[56] The details of this attack need not concern us, for the thesis being developed here does not depend upon the outcome. Suffice it to say that Eysenck and his colleagues basically contend that empirical studies do not on the whole show that persons in therapy matched with persons in control groups not in therapy get very much, if any, better than the controls. This contention has been disputed, and the matter is very far from being resolved at the present time.[57]

I have mentioned this controversy because it has become one of the factors in the decline in the prestige of dynamic psychology, even though the two are not directly related. That is, the dynamic understanding of personality could well contain much truth about man, and the psychotherapies related to it could still be ineffectual for a variety of reasons not related to the theory, such as poor therapists and poor therapeutic techniques. In point of fact it is now generally recognized that psychotherapy was overused as a treatment modality until recently. There are many kinds of difficulties for which "talk" therapy should not be the sole or central modality.[58]

Fortunately, there are several empirical studies that do tend to support a dynamic understanding of personality, at least in its essentials. These studies have been recently reviewed by Salvatore R. Maddi (who is himself not a dynamic theorist in this sense). Maddi found that the basic concept of unconscious defense mechanisms is well documented, particularly perceptual distortions related to repression and hypervigilance. Some of the Freudian conceptions of the stages of psychosexual development, particularly those relating to the anal stage, were well supported, though others less so.[59] The concept of unconscious defense is vital to my position, for the basic principle of compensation depends upon it, but other details are not so important to my general theory, however useful they may be in specific cases.

This brief discussion will suffice to establish the general credibility of the dynamic base of ego psychology. Now we must turn to the question of the ego per se.

Earlier, we noted the development of ego psychology out of classical psychoanalysis. The ego is viewed as having its own autonomy, and to some extent its own developmental pattern distinct from psychosexual development, though related to it. The best-known schema of the development of the ego is that of Erik Erikson.[60] Though Erikson's model has much to commend it, especially as a pioneering effort to extend Freud's basic model into adult life, its *epigenetic* principle leaves something to be desired. This principle indicates that the basic ground plan of the ego is there in "seed," as it were, and development is therefore basically a process of unfolding (that is, to be sure, the literal meaning of the term "development"). This view is subject to the same kinds of criticism applied to the blossom theories of health. It takes too little account of the freedom of the individual and the complexities of his interaction with the environment. In practice Erikson is very much aware of these factors, of course, for his experience as a clinician and observer stands him in good stead. Nevertheless, there is an alternative that is more useful.

Jane Loevinger has worked out a theory of ego development based upon a *hierarchical* principle rather than an epigenetic principle. That is, with every stage of ego development it increases in complexity of structure and function through its interaction with the environment, incorporating the functions of previous stages. She proposes six stages, ranging from presocial to integrated, each characterized by different forms of impulse control, interpersonal style, and conscious preoccupation.[61] These are not so clearly related to Freud's psychosexual schema as are Erikson's, nor do they cover in as great detail the whole life span, since "integrated" refers to the ego of a

mature adult of any age. But the basic principle is closer to
our best general understanding of development as proceeding
toward increased differentiation and subsequent reintegration,
and her language is not subject to the pejorative connotation
often given by psychodynamic concepts.

Characteristic of the mature ego is its strength and flexibility, enabling the person both to cope and to develop.
Loevinger rightly notes that criteria for positive mental health
offered by Marie Jahoda—namely, active adjustment, integration of personality, and perception free from need distortion
—are actually attributes of the mature ego.[62]

I believe that in beginning to describe health as a function
of the relative maturity of the ego, we do have a way of taking
into account the concreteness implied in the absence of impairment idea of health, the coping emphasis, and the emphasis on development offered by the blossom theory.

However, the relational emphasis at the center of the cultural approach is still missing. To get at this we must recall
the New Testament understanding of health as never being an
end in itself, but as related to salvation. Seward Hiltner has
rightly emphasized in his systematic, though brief, treatment
of the salvation-health relationship that the individual is not
the primary concern, but a derivative one, in the New Testament view. In this sense all modern theories are somewhat at
variance with the New Testament.[63] But the cultural approach
is perhaps closest to it in this regard, even though the splitting
off of mental and physical dimensions is unbiblical. Both it
and the New Testament are saying that we cannot finally
adequately define health *a se,* that is, in or of itself. Apart
from its relatedness, it has no specifiable identity. In the New
Testament, health has meaning as a part of the struggle between the powers of light and darkness. Its presence signals
an advance by the forces of light, and its loss, their retreat.

Although this does not quite add up to saying that health
is a quality that makes salvation possible in the New Testament, as we have noted in Chapter II, this does not appear to

be off target as a translation of the relationship from its original apocalyptic setting. There health participates in anticipatory fashion in the end-time, which for us means that it participates in the salvatory process which moves toward that end, as the all-important enabling factor. Without some degree of health, there can be no such participation.

Recognizing, then, that health has such a relational dimension, which provides it with its normative character, we can propose a formal definition of it. *Health generically refers to the relatively active potential for appropriate functioning which any individual possesses at any given time.* It is, then, the *enabling* factor that is present to some degree in everyone, not something that either is, or is not, present, as in the psychotherapeutic model which has been the basis of most of the discussion of the salvation-health relationship, as we have noted.

The term "appropriate functioning" is, of course, a formal and question-begging one. What is appropriate functioning? Appropriate for what? The necessity of answering this question confronts us again with the relational character of health. It can only be defined in relation to whatever is deemed appropriate, and not by itself. In the next chapter I shall present in some detail the kind of functioning I have in mind, but I must admit in advance that this will not be an "objective" discussion, since my values will inevitably play a major role— as anyone's values do in such discussions. To be sure, there are wide areas of agreement among health professionals about what is appropriate, but there are also some areas of disagreement. What, to suggest some examples, are the kinds of health that enable a person to construct bombs, to blow up buildings, hijack airplanes, torture prisoners, or ignore the plight of the poor? We shall be looking at these and other equally knotty questions. Meanwhile, let me simply say that by appropriate functioning I mean the ability to participate to some degree in the salvatory process, as I defined it in the preceding section.

Health is a factor possessed by *individuals* and not by groups. This will seem arbitrary to some, and it is certainly not intended to communicate that the health of individuals is something they have in isolation from others. I believe this has been made sufficiently clear. It may, of course, be used analogically to refer to groups large and small—thus we are accustomed to speak of healthy and unhealthy families, "sick" societies, and so on. However, such usage lacks the precision needed for our attempt to get a genuine and viable solution to the salvation-health question, and hence to the broader question of man's existence. Further, this usage runs some risk of subverting the central thing we are trying to understand, namely, the ways that the potential of the person can be actualized. By treating him fundamentally as a member of a group whose "health" is being discussed, inevitably we regard him to some extent as a part of the whole whose health is important basically as a contributing factor to the health of the group. However much the individual's sense of identity may depend upon his group membership, it is still *his* identity that is of primary value, not that of the group. Persons are the most complex organisms we know that have the capacity of experiencing or feeling (prehending). Hence it is they who have the greatest potential for participation in the salvatory process, and it is they whose health we are then concerned about.

Health refers to the individual's potential at *any given time*. This will, of course, to some extent vary from moment to moment, but my concern here is to limit our discussion of health to what is generally the current state of the individual. A person may have a good potential for appropriate functioning but at the same time be quite ill—with pneumonia, for example. Penicillin will bring about his recovery in a matter of days, but for the time being his degree of health, and hence his potential for functioning, is quite low. Likewise, a person may be in a state of acute depression and virtually immobilized, though appropriate therapeutic measures will relieve the depression in a few weeks' time. The potential is there but it is not active at that time, hence again the health state is low.[64]

I shall make no attempt to summarize this rather lengthy and perhaps even tedious discussion necessary to understand what is to follow. The reader who has survived to this point, however, may take heart—from here on I propose actually to do what I have been saying I have been preparing to do, that is, to present a model for understanding salvation and health.

NOTES

1. David E. Roberts, *Psychotherapy and a Christian View of Man* (Charles Scribner's Sons, 1950), p. 153.

2. Josef Goldbrunner, *Holiness Is Wholeness and Other Essays* (University of Notre Dame Press, 1964). The title essay was first given in lecture form ten years earlier, and so properly belongs to this period.

3. Seward Hiltner, *Preface to Pastoral Theology* (Abingdon Press, 1958), pp. 69, 89–115.

4. Albert C. Outler, *Psychotherapy and the Christian Message* (Harper & Brothers, 1954), pp. 43–44. It is not entirely clear in the book whether Outler regards psychotherapy or counseling based upon psychotherapeutic principles as an integral part of the salvatory process or not. But clearly he regarded it as having a useful place in the work of the ministry, and thus in some positive way related to salvation, much as man's natural knowledge provides a basis of revealed truth in the Thomistic position.

5. *The Relationship of the Christian Faith to Health* (General Assembly of The United Presbyterian Church U.S.A., 1960), pp. 15, 35–36. This pamphlet represented the careful work of an able committee, and did much to overcome resistance to healing ministries in the Presbyterian Church.

6. Eduard Thurneysen, *A Theology of Pastoral Care*, tr. by Jack A. Worthington and Thomas Wieser (John Knox Press, 1962). Published in Switzerland in 1957, this was the main statement

about pastoral theology from a Barthian perspective until Oden's work (see n. 15 below). It stressed the distinct difference between pastoral work and psychotherapy, though acknowledging that there is an analogy between the two (p. 240).

7. Daniel Day Williams, *The Minister and the Care of Souls* (Harper & Brothers, 1961).

8. *Ibid.*, pp. 26–27.

9. *Ibid.*, p. 28.

10. *Ibid.*, p. 27.

11. Williams' approach here is grounded in process philosophy, which also is basic to this present work. His book clearly reflected the relational character of this approach, but, in my judgment, does not spell out the relationship of salvation and health as this can and should be done. We can see clearly that compartmentalization of life is impossible through his work, but not so clearly that some distinctions need to be made in an operationally useful understanding of man.

12. Edward E. Thornton, *Theology and Pastoral Counseling* (Prentice-Hall, Inc., 1964).

13. *Ibid.*, pp. 70 f.

14. *Ibid.*

15. Thomas C. Oden, *Kerygma and Counseling: Toward a Covenant Ontology for Secular Psychotherapy* (The Westminster Press, 1966); *Contemporary Theology and Psychotherapy* (The Westminster Press, 1967).

16. Divine self-disclosure is a major theme of *Kerygma and Counseling,* especially Ch. II, and the "Cosmic Christ" is treated in *Contemporary Theology and Psychotherapy,* pp. 125 ff.

17. James N. Lapsley, "Kerygma and Counseling: A Review Article," *Journal of Pastoral Care,* Vol. XXI, No. 2 (June, 1967), pp. 100–103.

18. The analogy drawn for psychotherapy from the early history of the church is a rather surprising one—Gnosticism. The parallel is drawn between the worldly wisdom of Gnosticism and the secular healing of psychotherapy, both of which are partially effective approaches to man's woes, needing the corrective of the gospel for full understanding. In both cases the church feels free to use the language of the secular surrogate in order to communicate its message (Oden, *Contemporary Theology and Psychotherapy,* pp. 102–111).

19. As in the case of Outler (whom Oden regards as his most congenial predecessor; *Contemporary Theology and Psychotherapy*, p. 131), it is difficult to say finally to what extent psychotherapy and counseling are really salvatory. At points Oden suggests that there is something more to salvation than can be found in therapy, but in talking about this he uses the language of therapy with adverbs of intensification, e.g., "a deeper full-functioning enriched by God's own gracious functioning" (*Kerygma and Counseling*, p. 111). Again and again he points to revelation as the source of a complete *understanding* of these processes, as in the following passage: "Our discussion has implied . . . that effective psychotherapy is a *unique* process of self-disclosure and a special crystallization of empathetic understanding and unconditional positive regard, and that (more than other natural and historical processes) it often may actually mediate, concretize, and embody the divine forgiving love which is finally *clarified* [italics mine] once for all in Jesus Christ" (*Contemporary Theology and Psychotherapy*, p. 135). If only clarification is added by revelation, it appears that Oden has taken a Gnostic position himself with regard to the Christian faith. But perhaps this should not be pressed too far, since Oden has not specifically addressed the question of what more there is to salvation as process than is provided by psychotherapy.

20. Don S. Browning, *Atonement and Psychotherapy* (The Westminster Press, 1966).

21. Williams and Browning, both of whom draw upon a process conception of salvation, are partial exceptions to this statement. But neither of them explicates the implications of this for a contemporary view of salvation in the works we have studied. Williams does so in his *The Spirit and the Forms of Love* (Harper & Row, Publishers, Inc., 1968), but there he is not attempting to relate it to conceptions of health.

22. Seward Hiltner made one brief but systematic contribution to the literature on the salvation-health question in this period, "Salvation's Message About Health," *International Review of Missions*, Vol. LVII (1968), pp. 157–174. Since his position is so different from those I have discussed, and quite similar to my own, especially in its understanding of health, I shall deal with it in connection with my own constructive statement in Sec. 4 of this chapter.

23. Whitehead's principal systematic philosophical works are *Science and the Modern World* (London: The Macmillan Co., Ltd., 1926), *Religion in the Making* (London: The Macmillan Co., Ltd., 1926), and *Process and Reality* (London: The Macmillan Co., Ltd., 1929). Other works followed, but Whitehead's position did not change substantially after *Process and Reality*, his major theoretical treatise, and the central document of process philosophy. There are changes in the position from the first two named books to his last one, but in my discussion of Whitehead's position I shall refer generally to the shape it took there.

24. In his earlier works Whitehead tended to equate the terms "event" and "occasion," but in *Process and Reality* he distinguished them, and referred to an event as "a nexus of actual occasions inter-related in some determinate fashion in some extensive quantum" (p. 124). The idea of purpose relates primarily to the occasion and derivatively to the event or nexus. See John B. Cobb, Jr., *A Christian Natural Theology Based on the Thought of Alfred North Whitehead* (The Westminster Press, 1965), for an illuminating discussion (pp. 100 f.).

25. Whitehead, *Process and Reality*, p. 517.

26. *Ibid.*

27. *Ibid.*, p. 521. For a discussion of the relation of Whitehead's religious thought to the roots of his position in modern physics, see Ian F. Barbour, *Issues in Science and Religion* (Prentice-Hall, Inc., 1966).

28. Man's survival capabilities are related to the possibility of the existence of the "mental pole" of occasions apart from the "physical pole." See the discussion in Cobb, *op. cit.*, pp. 63 ff. Although Cobb interprets Whitehead as suggesting that the "mental pole" may exist without the physical pole, I do not think this is consonant with the great emphasis placed upon the psychophysical unity of events. Poles are not dualities. However, it could well be that the physical pole may exist in a subtle form not detectable by ordinary human perception, just as various kinds of electronic waves are not detectable. This is the hypothesis that seems to me most consistent with the evidence for survival. For a lucid and objective discussion of this evidence, see Rosalind Haywood's "Death and Physical Research," in Arnold J. Toynbee *et al.* (eds.), *Man's Concern with Death* (McGraw-Hill Book Company, Inc., 1969), pp. 219–250. Al-

though she does not consider the evidence overwhelming, there is a sufficient amount of it to force even the most skeptical to take the question of survival seriously. Although I do not think it is central to the question of salvation, it is of great interest to theologians concerned with the problem, and ought not to continue to be shunned as something alien to religion.

29. Browning, *Atonement and Psychotherapy*, p. 50.

30. The best guide to Pannenberg in English is *Theology as History*, Vol. III of New Frontiers in Theology, ed. by James M. Robinson and John B. Cobb, Jr. (Harper & Row, Publishers, Inc., 1967). This volume contains essays by Pannenberg, responses by American theologians, and interpretation by the editors. For an explicit discussion by Pannenberg of his position in relation to that of Whitehead, see Pannenberg, *Theology and the Kingdom of God*, ed. by Richard John Neuhaus (The Westminster Press, 1969), pp. 62, 65. He finds much of Whitehead compatible and illuminating, but rejects the idea of development in God (*ibid.*, p. 62).

31. Wolfhart Pannenberg, "The Revelation of God in Jesus of Nazareth," in Robinson and Cobb (eds.), *op. cit.*, Vol. III, p. 111.

32. *Ibid.*, p. 115. See also Kendrick Grobel's discussion, "Revelation and Resurrection," in the same volume (pp. 169–175). Grobel argues that the resurrection qualifies as an event in time, but not as an event in space, or if it does so, "only as a historically incredible event." Both he and Pannenberg point to I Cor., ch. 15, as the central text for light on the resurrection. In my view it is not necessary to look upon the resurrection as an incredible event, as there are in the history of religions many parallels to the experience of Paul on the Damascus road, which is cited by William Hamilton, "The Character of Pannenberg's Theology," in the same volume (p. 183), as the paradigm of Pannenberg's understanding of the resurrection, based upon a lecture that he gave at Vanderbilt University in April, 1963, entitled "Did Jesus Really Rise from the Dead?"

33. Pannenberg, "The Revelation of God in Jesus of Nazareth," p. 118.

34. Moltmann's two principal works translated into English are *Theology of Hope: On the Ground and Implications of a Chris-*

tian Eschatology, tr. by James W. Leitch (London: SCM Press, Ltd., 1967), and *Religion, Revolution, and the Future,* tr. by M. Douglas Meeks (Charles Scribner's Sons, 1969). In both works, Moltmann maintains a determined stance toward a narrow base in the New Testament eschatology, mostly omitting other sources of data. However, Daniel L. Migliore has shown that in other less well known writings Moltmann has taken a more open attitude toward certain other kinds of sources, notably in the field of politics ("The Theology of Hope in Perspective," *Princeton Seminary Bulletin,* Vol. LXI, No. 3 [Summer, 1968], pp. 42–50). Should this strand become dominant, we may, in fact, rightly regard Pannenberg and Moltmann as being on the same wavelength.

35. Daniel L. Migliore summed up the similarities and differences between process theology and the theology of hope (including the position of Pannenberg) in a lecture at Princeton Theological Seminary, March 24, 1969, as follows:

SIMILARITIES:

(1) Reality is processive, including nature, man, and God. God is internally involved in change, and influenced by it.

(2) There is an emphasis on creativity and the emergence of novelty.

(3) Society is viewed as organic, with creative self-giving seen as vital to its life.

(4) Special events function as revelatory and the Christ event is the decisive disclosure of the goal of history.

DIFFERENCES:

(1) Process theology is philosophically oriented, while the theology of hope is biblically oriented, though this is not an absolute difference.

(2) Process theology is teleologically oriented, while the theology of hope is eschatologically oriented. In the former, novelty is an extension of the given; in the latter, it is a surprise. The cross-resurrection paradigm in the theology of hope emphasizes the activity of God in the discontinuity and the coming of the new.

(3) In the area of politics, process theology is inclined toward liberalism, while the theology of hope inclines toward political radicalism. This is not an absolute difference, but relatively the former emphasizes beauty and the latter goodness, the former compromise and the latter confrontation.

I believe this is a useful summary account, although I disagree with the last point stated, and hold that process theology does not have any direct affinity to any political ideology.

Although the idea of the future as containing elements of discontinuity and surprise is not characteristic of process thinking, nevertheless Whitehead attempted to deal with the issue of risk involved in the creative advance under the category of "adventure." By adventure he meant the willingness to give up value in the present for the possibility of realizing value in the future, with attendant risks (*Adventures of Ideas* [The Macmillan Company, 1933], pp. 354, 357–361). Admittedly, however, this concept does not entirely overcome the lack of urgency in process thinking, unless coupled with some conception of the participation of the present in the future, such as Pannenberg's "prolepsis," which has been discussed.

36. See, e.g., Herbert E. Anderson, "Christian Baptism and the Human Life Cycle" (unpublished dissertation, Drew University, 1970). Anderson presents a view of sanctification closely related to Erik Erikson's "epigenetic" view of development, concluding that "sanctification is a life-long process that unfolds the meaning of baptism at phases and in a way that corresponds to more recent definitions of the human life cycle" (p. 372). He does not deal with the wider question of the relation of this to salvation.

37. The idea of beauty as central to ethics is, of course, not a new one in the history of theology. Jonathan Edwards, for instance, used it as a key idea in his *The Nature of True Virtue* (University of Michigan Press, 1960). See also *Coming To: A Theology of Beauty*, by William D. Dean (The Westminster Press, 1972).

38. At points Whitehead suggests that not only the values of the world but also the evil in it is preserved in the life of God, and transmuted somehow into good (*Religion in the Making*, p. 155, and *Process and Reality*, p. 525). A close reading of the latter text suggests an alternative reading, namely, that the *conse-*

quences of evil which contributed to the satisfaction of aims will be preserved, not the evil itself. "The Revolts of destructive evil, purely self-regarding, are dismissed into their triviality of merely individual facts; and yet the good they did achieve in individual joy, in individual sorrow, in the introduction of needed contrast, is yet saved by its relation to the completed whole." This alternative seems better to fit with Whitehead's conception of evil as mutual obstructiveness. Evil has no character of its own except negation.

39. Whitehead, *Process and Reality*, p. 532.
40. Charles Hartshorne, *Reality as Social Process: Studies in Metaphysics and Religion* (Free Press, 1953), p. 120.
41. For a somewhat detailed review of the situation at the beginning of the decade of the 1960's, see my "A Conceptualization of Health in Psychiatry," *Bulletin of the Menninger Clinic*, Vol. XVI, No. 4 (July, 1962), pp. 161–177.
42. Bernard Rimland, "Psychogenesis Versus Biogenesis: The Issues and the Evidence," in Stanley C. Plog and Robert B. Edgerton (eds.), *Changing Perspectives in Mental Illness* (Holt, Rinehart and Winston, Inc., 1969), pp. 702–735.
43. One cannot make detailed use of a theory that is largely empty of content as a basis of treatment, which means that most organically oriented psychiatrists must "fly by the seats of their pants" or rely on the empirical tests run on various drugs which show *that* they have certain effects, though *not* why they have them.
44. Karl A. Menninger, Paul W. Pruyser, Martin Mayman, *The Vital Balance: The Life Process in Mental Health and Illness* (The Viking Press, 1963). Crude "adjustment" versions of coping theory are no longer taken seriously by professionals.
45. Many psychoanalysts, including prominently Anna Freud, Ernst Kris, and Heinz Hartmann, as well as the psychologist David Rapaport, have contributed to the development of ego psychology. The central source in book form is Hartmann's *Ego Psychology and the Problem of Adaptation*, tr. by David Rapaport (International Universities Press, Inc., 1958).
46. Walter B. Cannon, *The Wisdom of the Body* (W. W. Norton & Company, Inc., 1939). The question of homeostasis is actually a rather complicated one, though its treatment as the central

idea in a view of human functioning oriented toward maintenance seems justified.

Closely related to it in Menninger's discussion is the concept
of *heterostasis* (literally, "standing other"). Here we find more
long-term endeavors to maintain the inner and outer environments, such as "falling in love, riding a hobby-horse, learning a
trade" (Menninger *et al., op. cit.,* p. 84). The term "steady state"
introduced by the theoretical biologist Ludwig von Bertalanffy
includes both homeostatic and heterostatic processes. It is a
relatively unsteady "steady state" characteristic of "open systems,"
that is, systems involved in a free exchange of energy with the
environment. Like all living things, man is such an open system,
though some part processes are relatively closed, such as the
regulation of the supply of salt in the blood (Menninger *et al.,
op. cit.,* pp. 92–93).

It should be noted, however, that von Bertalanffy does not
regard the "steady state" as a purely maintenance phenomenon,
but as the principle also underlying development. It is the "contradiction" in living things to the second law of thermodynamics
—the law of entropy, or the dissipation of energy. He holds that
the law of entropy does not apply to open systems. Though
eschewing a vitalistic teleology, he asserts that "living organisms
maintain themselves in a fantastically improbable state, preserve
their order in spite of continuous irreversible processes and even
proceed, in embryonic development and evolution, toward ever
higher differentiations" (*General System Theory: Essays on Its
Foundation and Development,* p. 159; George Braziller, 1969).
As will be spelled out in the text, I hold that the principle of
development described here is equally vital to an understanding of health as the principle of maintenance. Von Bertalanffy
rightly notes that system theory in the United States is dominated by the cybernetic approach, which has limited application to open systems such as man (*General System Theory,* p.
161).

47. The case of the assassin Sirhan Sirhan is a dramatic illustra-
tion of this point. According to Bernard L. Diamond, noted
forensic psychiatrist, Sirhan killed Robert Kennedy in a kind of
fugue triggered by alcohol and flashing lights, but underlying
was his deep love-hate for his father displaced onto Kennedy.

Though the jury did not believe this kind of evidence in this case of the death of a public figure, in other cases, notably in *People vs. Gorshen,* 1959, Diamond has been able to stimulate significant changes in the California law in the direction of recognizing unconscious, compensatory motivation (Bernard L. Diamond, "Sirhan B. Sirhan's Bizarre Paranoia," *Psychology Today,* Vol. III, No. 4 [September, 1969], pp. 48–55).

48. This is essentially the position of Salvatore R. Maddi, for instance. Maddi is a "consistency" personality theorist, holding that everyone seeks a certain consistent level of activation to which he has become accustomed. Development is a result of anticipated disturbances to this level. (*Personality Theories: A Comparative Analysis,* pp. 139–143; The Dorsey Press, Inc., 1968.) It appears also to be the position of Menninger *et al.* (*op. cit.,* p. 83), as we have noted, though they are not quite as explicit as is Maddi.

49. Carl R. Rogers, *Client Centered Therapy* (Houghton Mifflin Company, 1950); Abraham Maslow, "Some Basic Propositions of a Growth and Self-actualization Psychology," *Perceiving, Behaving, Becoming: A New Focus for Education* (Washington, D.C.: Yearbook of the Association for Supervision and Curriculum Development, 1962); Erich Fromm, *Man for Himself* (Rinehart & Co., Inc., 1947); Karen Horney, *Neurosis and Human Growth* (W. W. Norton & Company, Inc., 1950).

50. C. G. Jung also has taken a self-actualization approach in many of his writings, e.g., "On the Nature of the Psyche," *Collected Works,* tr. by R. F. C. Hull (Bollingen Series, Vol. XX; Pantheon Books, Inc., 1960), Vol. VIII, p. 223 *et passim.* Elsewhere, however, he has indicated that self-actualization, or "individuation," is only for the elite who can get psychotherapy. The masses must get what they can from symbolization and ritual to maintain a balanced psyche. See, e.g., "Psychology and Religion," *Psychology and Religion: West and East, Collected Works,* Vol. XI, p. 43 *et passim.* Hence he seems actually to favor a coping view of health, at least for most persons. Even those capable of engaging in psychotherapy are seen as facing intrapsychic conflict resulting from an imbalance of psychic forces.

51. Arthur Koestler has offered a brilliant exposition of the argument for tension between man's "lower" and "higher" psychic

functions in his *The Ghost in the Machine* (The Macmillan Company, 1967).

52. James N. Lapsley, *The Concept of Willing* (Abingdon Press, 1967), pp. 186–187.

53. Thomas S. Szasz, *The Myth of Mental Illness: Foundations of a Theory of Personal Conduct* (A Hoeber-Harper Book, Harper & Brothers, 1961); Theodore R. Sarbin, "Theoretical Perspectives," in Plog and Edgerton (eds.), *op. cit.*, pp. 9–30.

54. Herbert Barry, III, "Cultural Variations in the Development of Mental Illness," in Plog and Edgerton (eds.), *op. cit.*, pp. 155–178.

55. Franz Alexander, Thomas M. French, and George H. Pollock (eds.), *Experimental Studies and Results,* Vol. I of *Psychosomatic Specificity* (The University of Chicago Press, 1968). This volume reports on fourteen years of research at the Chicago Institute for Psychoanalysis. Although inconclusive in some respects, it establishes beyond a shadow of a doubt the role of psychic factors in some diseases.

56. Hans J. Eysenck, "The Effects of Psychotherapy: An Evaluation," *Journal of Consulting Psychology,* Vol. 16 (1952), pp. 319–324. In recent years this attack has been vigorously pursued by behavior therapists such as Joseph Wolpe and Cyril Franks.

57. See, for examples, Allen E. Bergen, "The Effects of Psychotherapy: Negative Results Revisited," and G. R. Pascal and Melvin Zax, "Psychotherapeutics: Success or Failure?"—both found in Arnold P. Goldstein and Sanford J. Dean (eds.), *The Investigation of Psychotherapy: Commentaries and Readings* (John Wiley & Sons, Inc., 1966), pp. 160–171. The former presents a rather strong case that at least some psychotherapy is effective, while the latter reports on the apparent effectiveness of therapy done at the University of Tennessee Counseling Service, though no experimental design was involved.

58. Drugs are the central treatment modality in an increasing number of cases as their effectiveness increases, and "symbolic" therapies, in which the power of symbols on the mind is central, continue to be of use. Such procedures as suggestion, hypnosis, and induced "conversion" are examples.

59. Maddi, *op. cit.*, pp. 174, 379–392.

60. Erik H. Erikson, *Childhood and Society* (W. W. Norton & Company, Inc., 1950).
61. Jane Loevinger, "The Meaning and Measurement of Ego Development," *American Psychologist,* Vol. 21, pp. 195–206. Loevinger's complete schematization of ego development is as follows:

STAGE	IMPULSE CONTROL AND CHARACTER DEVELOPMENT	INTERPERSONAL STYLE	CONSCIOUS PREOCCUPATION
Impulse ridden	Impulse ridden, fear of retaliation	Exploitative, dependent	Bodily feelings, especially sexual and aggressive feelings
Conformist	Conformity to external rules, shame	Exploitative, manipulative, zero-sum game	Things, appearance, reputation
Conscientious	Internalized rules, guilt	Intensive, responsible	Differences (?) inner feelings, achievements, traits
Autonomous	Coping with inner conflict, tolerating differences	Intensive concern for autonomy	Role conceptualization, development, fulfillment
Integrated	Reconciling inner conflicts, renunciation of the unattainable	Human individuality	Identity

I believe this to be a very useful scheme, although I shall be using the term "identity" in a somewhat broader sense than conscious preoccupation.

62. Marie Jahoda, *Current Concepts of Positive Mental Health* (Basic Books, Inc., 1958), pp. 71–72.
63. Hiltner, "Salvation's Message About Health." The conception of health as an "enabling" value presented by Hiltner in this article is very close to that developed in this book, though he

does not elaborate it. His conception of salvation, however, is more traditional, and focused on the individual.

64. I first presented this basic idea in "The Minister's Concern with Health," *Christian Advocate*, Vol. IV, No. 16 (Aug. 4, 1960), pp. 7–8. It has been considerably elaborated and developed since that time.

Chapter IV

A Dynamic Process Model
for Relating Salvation and Health

1. Factors

As indicated in the subtitle of the book, salvation and health are "interlocking" processes. By the term "interlocking" I mean that, though they can be analyzed and understood separately as has been shown, they are inseparable in actual occurrence, and mutually dependent in some respects. Further, their relationship will be shown to vary according to the dynamics of three key factors in the relationship: *development, maintenance,* and *participation.* That is, the relationship between salvation and health in any given person can be identified by understanding the interaction of these three factors. Since we have described health as an *enabling* quality and salvation as the process that it undergirds, our model will be a hierarchical one. That is, six levels of interaction among the three factors will be described, proceeding from very little participation in the salvatory process to as full participation as human beings are capable of. Thus participation in the salvatory process is the *criterion* upon which this model is constructed. This is appropriate for ministers whose primary discipline is theology, though members of the health professions might prefer a model based upon health as the final criterion.

The ideas of development and maintenance have already been sketched in Chapter III in connection with the discussion of modern conceptions of health, but it is necessary to say a bit more about them in order to understand how they are to be used in the model.

Development literally means an "unfolding," as the blossom theory of health suggests. Although it does certainly involve such an unfolding, and is composed almost entirely of this working out of an inner ground plan in embryonic and seminal stages, it involves much more than that in later stages, even in relatively primitive organisms. In "open systems" (i.e., living things), complex interchanges with the environment mean that development takes place partly in response to these processes, even though the direction and goal of development may remain the same.[1] Who has not been impressed by the sight of a tree trunk bent by the wind yet reaching for the sun and sky with its branches? As was noted in Chapter III, some of this adaptive development may be called compensatory; that is, it occurs in order to make up for some lack, either physical or emotionally felt. The camel's hump which has become a part of a whole species is a clear example of compensation for the scarcity of water in the desert. But compensation also plays a role in many individual human lives if, indeed, not in all.

Yet development into new levels of complexity cannot exhaustively be described under the notion of compensation. Von Bertalanffy's conception of the "steady state," toward which organisms in an unstable condition tend, appears to be clearly one element in understanding noncompensatory development.[2] But one does not have to be a romantic idealist as Tennyson was in "Ulysses" to find man often becoming restless in seemingly stable and steady states and overturning them in stressful enterprises.[3] Here the steady state idea seems inadequate, unless stretched into an unrecognizable shape. Some other principle must be added to understand the strivings of some men, at least. Here the conception of the "lure" of God, which has been discussed, can help us, and we shall be making considerable use of it, especially in discussing some levels of the salvation-health relationship.[4]

As discussed in the previous chapter, my references to the

concept of development will refer primarily, though not ex-
clusively, to ego development, and in particular to the model
presented by Jane Loevinger.[5] For it is upon the vicissitudes
of the ego in its struggles to cope, defend, and actualize that
our attention will be focused.

Maintenance of a relatively stable equilibrium is a primary
task of every organism, as we have seen, even though it is
constantly changing its physical composition. Though there
are obviously numerous physiochemical processes and systems
involved in the maintenance of persons, the primary psychic
factors are relatively few. I hold that they can essentially be
reduced to a *sense of worth* and a *sense of identity*. These are
the two personal characteristics without which a human being
cannot long exist, and which to preserve and enhance he will
often go to any lengths.[6]

By a sense of worth I mean the individual's estimate of himself in comparison to some standard of excellence, whether
this is conscious or unconscious, articulated or unarticulated
—and it is usually partly all of these. His estimate does not
have to be as high as the standard, necessarily, for him to be
comfortably maintained. But it must not fall too low or he
will begin to take some form of action to restore the balance.
The level below which it cannot fall without such action being
taken depends upon how vital a part of his *identity* the standard is. In some cases he cannot too closely approximate the
level of the standard either, lest his identity be violated. In
the era now coming to a close young women often had difficulty in acknowledging their intellectual abilities (even
though they thought that some brains were all right), lest
their identities as female, hence weak and emotional, be
threatened. These standards are usually in complex relationship to one another as well as to the sense of identity, neces-
sitating constant adjustment in order to maintain equilibrium.
In cases where the standards are approximated, however,
these adjustments require little conscious or even unconscious
effort and energy.

Identity, in the broad sense in which I am employing it, is a part of the person from the earliest months of life, though it does not take on central significance until the individual is able to distinguish himself from his environment and to have some sense of gender. After that it comes to include not only his physical body but also his immediate life space, his clothing, his room, his toys. Identity, then, includes the specific focus of adolescence and postadolescence discussed by Erikson and Loevinger, and also later manifestations, such as the need for integrity in old age, as discussed by Erikson.[7] Another way to put it is to say that the individual must have a sense of selfhood, but the term "self" has taken on so much ambiguity that it seems less useful than the term "identity," which has the advantage of stressing the core factor of integrity of personality which must be protected at whatever cost. Disintegration is a fear that lies behind many human actions that otherwise seem bizarre, and many that do not, since they are widely shared, such as ritual behavior.[8]

Development and maintenance are to a certain extent polar factors in the health-salvation relationship. Development beyond the earliest stages always brings some risk that maintenance will be lost and equilibrium permanently upset. The self, with its need for worth and identity, is reluctant to risk itself in developmental ventures. This is especially true as higher levels of maintenance have been reached. One must be willing to take a *transpropriate* risk (literally, "beyond the self") in order to continue development and avoid fixation.[9] On the other hand, too rapid development in some directions can indeed upset one's balance, and does so at the onset of puberty. Hence the temptation is to use development to maintain one's balance, rather than risk losing it—as does the young man who overdevelops his torso by weight lifting.

As the ego matures, however, and the person becomes more flexible and integrated, the tension between maintenance and development considerably lessens, and this lessening makes possible increased *participation*. Participation must be under-

stood more literally than we are accustomed to regard it if
its meaning is to be clear in this discussion. Usually we think
of participation as individuals collectively engaged in some
activity, such as a team sport, to achieve some effect jointly
that they could not achieve individually. While this "aggre-
gate" conception of participation is not wholly wrong, in that
each individual retains his identity, it misses the fundamental
truth that these individuals are literally involved in a common
life to which they contribute or "influence." Something from
their lives does actually flow into the others from a process
point of view. They give of themselves to the lives of those
with whom they participate, and to some extent literally become a part of them. Marriage is the human relationship in
which this is most obvious, not only because of the physical
attachment and internal "prehension," but also because of
the rapport that builds up over the years in many marriages,
even when this has a negative valence.

Such is the nature of participation in a view of reality that
takes relationship as a primary category. This does not mean,
though, that all participation predominantly is salvatory in
character. It may be quite destructive, and all participation
is ambiguous to some extent, because of the inescapability of
some evil effects of even the best intentions. Nevertheless, increased development does make increased participation possible, and where this development is not primarily in the
service of maintenance, the possibility of significant participation in the salvatory process is enhanced. Human freedom remains a variable that is not entirely predictable, however, so
there is no guarantee that increased health, now being seen,
and the ability to participate will automatically lead to salvation. It provides for the possibility and, at most, for some pre-
disposition toward such participation.

This, then, is a description of the factors in the salvation-
health model being proposed, and a general sketch of how
they are related. I shall now present the model in detail, de-
scribing six levels of relationship, proceeding from the least
possibility for salvatory participation to the greatest.[10]

2. The Hierarchical Model

In this section I shall attempt to describe each level of the salvation-health relationship in sufficient detail and concreteness to identify clearly persons whose patterns of living approximate it. Like all models and typologies, correspondence with reality will be only approximate, and caution must always be exercised lest persons become permanently "fitted" into some level which is at best a temporary descriptive and heuristic device to aid in responsible decision-making.

Level One. This first level is dominated by maintenance dynamics. There is little or no development or participation in the sense described above as active contribution. Life processes are concentrated upon maintaining the unsteady equilibrium which characterizes this level, or upon regaining it if it has been lost, as in the crisis of a serious illness.

The prototypes of this level are the newborn and the terminally ill. Both are almost totally dependent upon their human and nonhuman environment to maintain life. They do not have resources to give much in return. Their capacity for participation, and hence for salvatory participation, is very minimal. Others in this situation are those critically ill physically or mentally (such as an acute schizophrenic reaction), those suffering from extreme mental and emotional retardation, those in acute grief or emotional shock, and those seriously injured in accidents or warfare.

In most cases the organism has suffered some physical trauma which has caused it to mobilize all its resources to combat the trauma. In the case of severe mental and emotional disturbances, we find a combination of psychic and physical factors producing the trauma, in all likelihood. Though schizophrenia now seems clearly related to some organic factors, it seems just as clearly related to psychic factors—the severe breakdown of the sense of identity, and, to a somewhat lesser extent, of the sense of worth. In cases of severe depression the reverse is the case. The sense of worth is shattered completely and the sense of identity somewhat less so. In cases of severe autism in children the causes are still not well understood, but in all probability a combination of physical and psychic factors is involved.

Does not this amount to saying that such persons are actually outside the ambit of God's grace? Does it not mean that they are not being saved? And if so, is this not an intolerable position for a Christian?

Let us recall that from the point of view of process theology, personhood, and not personal entities, are finally saved, though persons participate in the salvatory process. It is true that persons at the maintenance level, then, are not participating to a great degree in this process, but this does not mean that God is unconcerned about them. Rather, it means that some of them are victims of the tragic limitations of existence as we know it, and the inevitability of evil. In the case of those about to die after living a full participatory life the tragedy is minimal, for they have already given what they have to give. For the newborn, there is no tragedy at all if they survive and develop. And for those in the crisis of illness, the experience may even have its constructive aspects, as many return from such an acute siege with a new vision of their lives and renewed purpose. But for the severely handicapped in mind and body the tragedy of their predicament is real, and what they might have been will never be. For those cut off by death, it is the same, except that with them all attempts even at maintenance fail also.

In concluding the description of this level I must point out that not even the most severely crippled or comatose person is completely without ability to participate in the salvatory process. Those familiar with the hospital ministry know that the very ill and dying have much to teach and much to give to those who have ears to hear and eyes to see, especially if they have become sensitive to nonverbal aspects of communication. Even the seemingly hostile and withdrawn emotionally disturbed child seeks in his own groping way to participate, and will respond to those who have the patience and skill. Those who have worked in mental hospitals know that to enter the strange and terrifying world of the schizophrenic is a frightening experience, but one that may help that sufferer to reach out and respond. Though modern tranquilizing drugs have largely eliminated the more bizarre aspects of this experience—such as the use of bodily excrement as a means of communication—the isolation and the quiet terror remain. R. D. Laing, the British psychoanalyst, has even been urging that those suffering from schizophrenia may be in truer touch with reality than those of us who are not.[11] While I think this is an extreme position, it is true that many so-called schizophrenics are persons of great sensitivity and perceptiveness (perhaps too much for the world in which they find themselves), from whom we can gain much by participating in *their* world.

So, then, all, or almost all, have something to offer and can participate to some extent. But it is up to those who have much greater capacities to help them to do so. And a hard look at those whose lives are lived out at the maintenance level can only bring to us a depth of awareness of the tragedy and suffering which is integral to the world we know. Yet God suffers with them "with groanings which cannot be uttered."

Level Two. At this level the accent is on development as the primary life orientation, alternating with maintenance for briefer periods of time. Participation is largely restricted to learning and play, for this is the level at which "normal" children and early adolescents live. It is a level characterized much more by receiving than by giving, though, of course, some giving does occur, as parents and teachers will agree.

This level is not restricted to childhood, however, for adults "retooling" or reorienting themselves will also exhibit these characteristics. Their "participation" is largely in the service of development, and quite consciously so.

With children the situation is often different. For them participation is real at the conscious level. A child is not aware that his games are a kind of dry run for living; for him they *are* living. We are generally aware of this in small children and regard their make-believe behavior as quite normal. We often forget that the same applies to a lesser extent to adolescence, however. A glance at the stages of ego development presented by Loevinger (n. 61, Chapter III, above) will show us that an intense concern for autonomy (stage five) characterizes adolescence, which often results in what appears to be pathological resistance to all kinds of authority. In our contemporary society this is, of course, intensified by the so-called generation gap, and the undeniably extreme tension existing between young people and the older generations. But it existed before these recent unfortunate developments in our culture, as it does to some extent in every culture. Young people must come somehow to sense that they are free and able to stand on their own two feet. Some cultures have elaborate rites of passage for this purpose, including various trials and initiation rites. For some of our young people, street demonstrations serve this purpose, among others.

The reader may have at least a couple of questions about this level. The first is, if this is normal, how can one distinguish it from what is abnormal? In approaching this question we must remember that health is always a matter of degree, and that our question really is whether the behavior we observe is appropriate or inappropriate, and if it is inappropriate, does the person concerned have the ability to behave appropriately if conditions are altered somewhat? The conditions of existence for young people in our culture are quite stressful. We expect them to behave like adults while on the whole treating them as children. They see our society as life with dehumanizing competition and injustice, and resist our insistence that they participate in it. When they become violent or quite withdrawn, their behavior may be regarded as inappropriate, but a change in the outlook of our society may well produce changes in a benign direction.

On the other hand, some young people, because of personality disturbances originating earlier in childhood while the ego was being formed, are not able to behave appropriately under almost any circumstances, and need special help. Their "participation" may really be in the service of maintenance rather than developmental tasks. Boys get the feeling of power from football and/or hot rods, and girls get the feeling of being wanted from promiscuous sexual relations in order to sustain their senses of identity and worth at tolerable levels. Perseveration in inappropriate behavior through changing circumstances is one way of determining whether the behavior is developmentally or maintenance oriented; the latter persevere. Clinical interviews and/or psychological testing by those skilled in such procedures may be very helpful, though seldom definitive.

The other question that may well have occurred to the thoughtful reader is, If children, young people, and even adults who are retooling are relatively "healthy," why are they discussed in connection with such a low level on the salvation-health continuum? If the model were a model of degrees of health, they would have to get a rather high level of designation. But it is a model of the salvation-health relationship in which salvation, not health, is the final criterion. Health as the enabling factor at this level is primarily directed at development, not at participation.

Participation is engaged in mostly for learning and developing, as we noted, though as in Level One, some salvatory participation not only is possible but does in fact take place from very early childhood onward. Anyone who has had experience with young children knows that they have much to offer— some of it exasperating, but some of it uniquely personal and meaningful. They spontaneously participate in the stream of life, and some of it becomes a permanent part of those about them who have the grace to learn from the naïve wisdom of children.

At this level we note for the first time that there is not a one-to-one correlation between health and salvation, so that we cannot say with assurance that where we find the one, the other will be present in roughly the same degree. Here we can see our way beyond the general positive correlations that have characterized earlier discussions to a more discriminating position. This tension between health and salvation will become even more acute in the next two levels before we find them once again positively correlated in the last two. This tension will, however, be the reverse of that which we have just noted in Level Two. For in Levels Three and Four we find that a lesser degree of health may make possible relatively greater participation in the salvatory process.

Level Three. At this level we find the principle of *compensation* playing a dominant role, with participation and development compensating the person for felt inadequacies at the maintenance level, or preventing the occurrence of such felt inadequacy. Here we find perhaps the majority of our whole adult population. The conditions of existence in our society (and perhaps in all societies to date) are such that most persons attain only a relatively unstable and vulnerable level of ego development. This level can be maintained, then, only by various devices employed to prevent the slipping or eroding of this level. These coping devices are more or less costly to the individual and those about him. Since they are always designed to protect the senses of identity and worth, they have as their primary cost the prevention of development, except as it may serve to secure the maintenance level. Minutemen and others have developed considerable skill with small arms, but this development is in the service of maintaining and enhancing their identity and worth as 100 percent Americans. For a "conflict free" sphere of the ego to function, there must be less than total preoccupation with maintenance, and such a sphere is needed for free development.

Relatively less costly devices employed by many persons include conformity to one's peer group in matters of dress, taste, transportation, belief, speech patterns, and general demeanor. These devices are designed to ward off a sense of *shame,* which includes both a fear of being exposed and a fear of being excluded from the group and thus having one's identity disconfirmed.

A second type of coping device commonly found in our culture which focuses on maintenance is that which is designed to allay or prevent feelings of guilt. Gifts of time and money to churches, schools, and charitable institutions are often rooted in such a need (though not always), and sometimes career choice itself is strongly related to it—especially in the service professions, though not restricted to them. It is principally because of this type of coping that maintenance by compensation has a relatively high position on the salvation-health model. Whatever our opinion of this kind of motivation, it is undeniable that many persons whose personality dynamics involve a strong guilt component (often largely or even entirely unconscious) have made great contributions to our society. These contributions have been real and their effects in aiding the development and participation of others incalculable. Many would argue, in fact, that this is the other side of the so-called Protestant ethic. One works to achieve wealth and hence worth and identity, but then one must give some of it away in order to maintain one's balance. This latter phenomenon has, of course, been much more prominent a feature of the second and third generation in families of great wealth, but not absent in the first. Though this whole orientation to life appears to be definitely losing ground in our culture, there are still many persons for whom it is a central element in their life-styles. Their central concern is to prevent the feeling of "badness" from becoming dominant in their self-experience. Though in the history of the race guilt feelings may well be rooted in fear of mutilation as Freud supposed, in the experience of most adults for whom it is important it is probably rooted in the more generalized fear of disintegration in which both identity and worth would, of course, be lost.

Another coping device that may be used in combination

with either of the above or without them, especially in cases of severely fixated development, is that of ego constriction. Basically this is a very cautious orientation to life that attempts to reduce all risks to a bare minimum, and hence participation other than that with which one is quite familiar. Ego constriction puts a limit on the quality of participation that a person operating at Level Three may attain, since it prevents his taking a flexible approach to his involvement. Sometimes such constriction is referred to as rigidity of character, and in communities which value relatively low-cost maintenance as a desired achievement, such rigidity may be understood as strength of character and prized. Though we may be tempted to scorn such an orientation as far less than optimal, it may well be all that many persons can achieve, and seems to have been a foundational psychosocial characteristic of civilization thus far. In unstable social situations, such as the one we currently face, it tends to become inappropriate and often contributes to the destruction of potential values.

Turning now to more costly attempts at maintenance by compensatory participation and/or development, we find two variations on conflicted behavior—one focally intrapersonal and interpersonal, the other psychosocial. The first we may call neurotic, understood in the usual sense in which the term is used to denote behavior which is a result of intrapsychic conflict and the fear and anxiety accompanying it. The classical obsessional neurosis may be taken as an example. In this affliction the victim experiences extreme discomfort rooted in guilt and shame associated with the discharge of excrement if his life is not always neat, orderly, and arranged in just the right way. By keeping it so he is able to ward off the feelings of guilt and/or shame and the anxiety attendant upon them, and also saves himself from the contrary desire to be messy, an even greater threat. The devices that he uses to accomplish this are relatively costly in time and energy, whether they take the form of excessive cleaning and straightening, or ritual behavior that appears to have no intrinsic relationship to the underlying problem. We can see clearly the difference between such a coping device and those discussed above as being less costly, in that they are on the whole adaptive to the environment in which the person finds himself. Not so with the person afflicted with a neurosis, for he must spend much of his energy "participating" in activity that has meaning only to himself, thus largely precluding his more constructive efforts in other directions. To be sure, many persons, if not most, experience some internal conflict that results in some neurotic behavior, but this is rather minimal in most cases and does not constitute a principal coping device.

The more costly *psychosocial* device for maintaining one's level of ego development is generally called prejudice. Prejudice is a virtually universal human phenomenon, and contrary to the popular lyric from *South Pacific*, "Carefully Taught," probably doesn't have to be taught, though teaching certainly reinforces, directs, and intensifies it. The most common form in our culture is, of course, ethnic prejudice. Admittedly, the roots of prejudice are still not fully understood. One source that seems rather clear is the need that the young child has to get a clear picture of himself (which also seems to be shared by the higher animals) to which his senses of identity and worth can be attached and developed. Other children who are both very much *like* him, and yet in some ways strikingly different, are disturbing to the clarity of this picture. He asks himself (nonverbally) some such question as this: "If they are all right, then is something the matter with me? No. Something must be the matter with them." In this way the child overcomes his initial fright in the presence of the similar yet different creature (which I have observed personally). His "prejudice" then may be more or less reinforced by his identification with his ethnic peer group, adult attitudes, and social patterns of segregation which suggest that, indeed, something must have been wrong with *them*, since he is not allowed to associate with them. It can be overcome early in its specific manifestations by proper adult attitudes and integrated school and play situations. However, most persons retain a rather strong prejudice potential in the presence of previously unknown similar but different persons, unless they have developed beyond the compensated maintenance level.

The power of ethnocentrism has recently and frighteningly been the subject of a careful study of voting patterns by Kevin P. Phillips.[12] Though Phillips' conclusion that the country is headed for thirty years of Republican rule may be questioned, his analysis of voting patterns reveals that not only do people tend to vote in ethnic blocs, but also that when they shift from one party to another, they tend to shift in blocs. These blocs reflect the peculiar prejudices of the ethnic groups involved, though economic and religious factors also play a part. Phillips' thesis that such blocs vote mainly *against* other blocs would be hard to substantiate fully, though hostility and grievances clearly play a large part.

My point in referring to this phenomenon is to show the power of prejudice as a maintenance device on a wide scale. Though political and economic factors play a part, they are subordinate to the need to maintain (and perhaps enhance) the senses of identity and worth. One meets the same phenomenon in the churches and local communities everywhere.

Though the cost of prejudice is usually not apparent to the individual, who, of course, does not even as a rule recognize it, its cost to the society as a whole is enormous, and therefore indirectly to the individual. Yet prejudiced participation is not without some salvatory effect on the "ingroup" at least, however damaging it may be to those in the "outgroup." The Irish in the United States have, over the past one hundred years, risen to full participation in our society, partly because of their fierce ingroup loyalty and prejudice against Yankees, Jews, Italians, and Germans. Today we may be witnessing the beginning of the same pilgrimage by the black people whose prejudice has considerable rational foundation. The question is whether our society can continue to withstand the trauma of progress through prejudice.

Although there are other recognizable high-cost coping de- vices in addition to neurosis and prejudice, such as alcoholism and other drug addictions, these two will serve to illustrate the central points in this type of coping.[13]

Yet another type of compensated maintenance, or attempt at coping, is the panic reaction. Violence of all sorts, when unplanned, falls into this category, and its general increase in our society shows the breakdown of less expensive means of maintaining identity and worth. Another form is the so-called acute schizophrenic reaction in which a deep regression sets in as an attempt to cope with a situation that is felt to be over- whelming. Though this fails as maintenance at one level, it may succeed at a more regressive level, even down to the nonparticipation of the catatonic who sits without moving, in which case the regression is to Level One on the present scale.

Another form of traditional panic reaction in our culture is the shotgun wedding, presumably becoming rare. But taking its place is the quickie illegal abortion. And behind both lie the often impulsive sexual relationships which are frequently a kind of maintenance device for both boys and girls, who need the experience as reassurance more than venereal pleas- ure. Although with changing mores in the direction of per- missiveness in the areas of both violence and sex they may become less used as maintenance "safety valves" to be turned on in panic, their deep roots in the most primitive aspects of man's life will continue to lend them a specially charged aura.

The extreme panic reaction is violence against oneself— suicide. Paradoxically most suicides are committed primarily in an attempt to preserve the identity and worth of the self, though such factors as isolation and inability to trust may have led to the extremity experienced in this regard. Suicidal gestures, on the other hand, are usually efforts to get others to recognize one's identity and worth.

This concludes my discussion of Level Three. Of all the levels discussed it is most clearly identifiable with the classical ego defenses described by psychoanalysis—repression, dis- placement, projection, perceptual distortion, and the other ego defenses.[14] Also here we find the psychosocial balancing mechanisms described by the sociologists who have investigated the mainstream of our culture. These generally give us a feeling of revulsion and disdain, but once again I must point out that they so far have carried the burden of civilization.

Level Four. The essential feature of life at this level of the salvation-health relationship is participation mainly for the sake of and in the service of development. Though somewhat similar to Level Two, in which development is the essential and obvious feature, it differs in that participation is a much more obvious feature and some investigation is required to discover that it is mainly in the service of development. Such participation is likely to be intense and to persevere over long periods of time—only to be rather suddenly terminated for no apparent reason. The actual reason in such cases is that the participation involved has served its developmental purpose. Such participation is nevertheless quite genuine in the sense that it is "meant" as more than a game, as the participation in Level Two is not. Its potential as salvatory is therefore much greater than that in Level Two. It provides more possibility for salvatory participation than does Level Three because persons at this level are relatively more flexible in their participation. They are freer to experiment to some extent and to improvise, because they are not bound to maintenance strategies by identity and worth quotients that are too low. To be sure, in some circumstances these factors will come into play, but they are not pervasive of the whole life-style as they are in Level Three.

This level is characteristic of "normal" young adults, though instances of it may be found among some adolescents and older adults. The former are precocious, not in the usual sense of having some hyperdeveloped skill which is actually compensatory in character, but in the sense of developing the personality toward mature humanity. The latter are experiencing development that has been delayed by environmental or personal factors—such as a crippling neurosis finally worked through in psychotherapy.

I shall take three aspects of young adulthood which actually interpenetrate in their pervasiveness and show how they can be understood as developmental participation. These are marriage, vocation, and morality.

Several recent studies have stressed the understanding of marriage as needed for the full development of the person. Indeed, Blanck and Blanck have argued that marriages undertaken for purposes other than development are bound to get into trouble.[15] This seems to be true of marriages undertaken for maintenance purposes where conflicting identity and worth needs inevitably lead to combat and eventual disruption, but not always true of marriages between mature individuals undertaken for companionate and sexual purposes. In our culture, people tend to marry in their early or mid twenties when they are in what is still, for many, late adolescence caused by prolonged education. Hence maintenance motives may often be mixed with developmental ones, producing conflict potential, but not so severe that it cannot be reduced by careful premarital counseling.

The focus of development in marriage is normally on the capacity for intimacy, empathy, and warmth. After this has been developed, the marriage must find another basis upon which to be sustained, either intrinsic, in which case the partners are deeply and genuinely attracted to each other as persons, or utilitarian, in which case they remain married for reasons of social and economic convenience.[16] The notion of romantic love is a cultural myth originating in the Middle Ages, when it served to alleviate some of the severe repression in the socially oriented marriages of aristocratic women. It did not then and does not now serve as a basis for marriage, despite well-nigh universal belief. Rather, it serves as a guise for the developmental function of marriage, which is seldom openly acknowledged. Such acknowledgment may well become more common in the future, however, as young people continue to gain more awareness of themselves. To be sure, marriage has other significant functions besides development —procreation, child-rearing, social control of sex. Yet its functioning depends significantly upon the success of the developmental dimension, and that is the only one which cannot be replaced by other social conventions, such as the *kibbutz* used in Israel for child-rearing. In the future it may well become the acknowledged foundation and principal justification for marriage.

In a marriage in which the capacity for intimacy, empathy, and warmth (treated here as one capacity with distinguishable elements) is significantly developed, a high quality of participation in the salvatory process is the result, for this capacity will come to characterize the relationship of the partners in appropriate ways outside the marriage. They become contributors to the general fund of beauty in the cosmic process, in both its human and divine aspects.

Not all development in marriage is of this sort, however. Some marriages are closer to being child-rearing arrangements in which one partner is attempting to bring up the other. I am familiar with one such marriage in which the wife succeeded in rearing her rather dependent, though intellectually gifted young husband. But when he "grew up" and lost some of his dependency, he realized that he had married his wife to get a mother, and marriage generated too much conflict to be sustained. Here necessary development of the ego toward autonomy was taking place, but it was not appropriate for marriage.

Other kinds of development that are not appropriate but that have wide credence in our culture are marriage to "settle down" a promiscuous young man or woman, or marriage to "make a man" of someone and get him to assume adult responsibility. Both of these have the cards stacked against them, for they are due to serious flaws in ego development which have resulted in costly maintenance patterns that cannot provide enough flexibility for successful marriages. Sometimes, of course, such marriages do succeed when the maintenance patterns are not fixed at too low an identity and worth quotient, and development can take place.

The area of *vocational choice* is one in which important intrapsychic as well as technical and interpersonal development is involved. Ordinarily we think of vocational choice as being related primarily to such things as skills and income expectation, and these are important. But equally important are the kinds of personal needs that are to be met in the vocation. Young men in our culture must come to some kind of terms with their complex set of feelings regarding their parents and their vocations—especially their fathers. This includes, of course, the expectations of the parents for their son's vocation. When these feelings are still intense and unresolved in late adolescence when vocational choice is usually made, they exert perhaps the determinative influence upon it. This results in the son following the father in the vocation, often to succeed only moderately, especially if his father succeeded only moderately. Or it may result in his choosing an entirely different line of work, even though he is well suited to something similar from the point of view of endowment.

While these may seem to be extreme examples (they occur often in "service" vocations, at least), they illustrate the role of personality dynamics and needs in vocational choice, and show how the development of ego autonomy and integrity are related to it. A vocation is the primary way in which one's identity and worth are finally confirmed at a high enough quotient so that their maintenance is not a constant conscious and unconscious concern—a confirmation that unfortunately does not take place in many cases.

If the vocational choice was a good one in terms of endowment, education, and opportunities, it eventually becomes "functionally autonomous," to use Gordon W. Allport's celebrated conception.[17] By this I mean that after the developmental task has been accomplished the vocation must have intrinsic meaning or the person will become quite restless in it, no matter how successful he may appear to be. The quality of his participation will suffer, and he will regress to the compensated maintenance level (Three). As in the case of marriage, vocational choice begun on the basis of developmental needs must be continued and completed on the basis of intrinsic participation.

Morality is, of course, a question pervasive of all of life, including the two vital areas just discussed. From the perspective of developmental participation, however, it has some distinctive features that can illuminate this discussion. Recently there have been several schemes of moral development proposed which have the common feature of viewing it as a progression from a punishment and power orientation through several stages, including mutual back-scratching, approval-seeking, obedience to fixed rules and authorities, to more universalistic and general codes stressing respect for human rights and equality.[18] These are based on sufficient cross-cultural, empirical studies for us to take them as more than merely armchair opinions.

Although most persons do not progress beyond the level of obedience to fixed rules and authorities, "law and order," an increasing number of young persons in our culture are doing so, another source of tension in the "generation gap." In order to get beyond it, many go through a stage of almost total rejection of the "law and order" values. But Laurence Kohlberg, who has made the study of morality his specialty, has found that young people do pass through this nihilistic stage. They develop their moral position until it reaches either what Kohlberg calls the "social-contract legalistic orientation," which stressed individual agreed-upon rights, or "universal ethical principle orientation," the highest of Kohlberg's six stages.

My point in this discussion is that the active social action orientation of many youth in the 1960's may be understood as developmental participation in which they are attempting to sharpen their own moral vision and experience as an aspect of identity. This point must not be overgeneralized, for, as has been noted, some young people are demonstrating as a kind of "game" and are operating basically at Level Two, and some have moved beyond the developmental stage or regressed to a precarious maintenance. The last-named possibility seems to be the case with the extremely alienated violent left whose identity and worth are intensely involved with the effort to destroy the established order.

The quality of participation in its moral dimension at this level possesses high potential for salvation, since moral commitments are intense. It also possesses high potential for destructiveness, and in the troubled times in which we live these two are close together at the behavioral moment of truth. If the developmental drive is paramount, however, the content and focus of the commitment are likely to vary considerably, and even to fade suddenly for no apparent reason.

In concluding this discussion of Level Four, developmental participation, we may note that, although a person may not develop in all the ways described at once—that is, he may be essentially at a maintenance level in one or more of them— if significant development is taking place, it tends to lend his whole life pattern a quality of openness and freedom from the constant necessity of protecting his identity and worth. His developmental involvement gives him enough of a sense of participating in something of importance both for him and for others that it "overflows," as it were, into other areas of his life, making the defensive coping devices discussed under Level Three less necessary.

Level Five. At this level we find a life pattern characterized mainly by participation for the sake of participation itself, though with some aspects for the sake of maintenance and development. This level is attained by only the relatively mature person whose major developmental tasks, discussed in Level Four, have been attained. He derives his satisfaction directly from his experience of participation and the anticipated results of such participation in his own life and the lives of others. To put this in the categories of process theology, he seeks the experience of beauty from his participation more than the reduction of tension arising from unmet maintenance and development needs. His subjective aim is toward the increase of beauty in his own life and the lives of others. Occasionally, circumstances arise in which maintenance and development need to play a major role, but this is not often.

In order to get a clearer picture of life patterns lived at this level, let us examine the life of John Woolman, the eighteenth-century American Quaker, who would certainly have been canonized long since if Quakers had official saints. Woolman is chiefly remembered today for his opposition to slavery in a society (mid-eighteenth-century New Jersey and Pennsylvania) that accepted it without much questioning. Not only was Woolman an outspoken opponent of slavery, but he was equally opposed to other forms of human suffering. Late in his life on a visit to England (where he died) he refused to ride in stagecoaches because of the hardships endured by the postboys who had to ride outside. This was typical of his response to such situations; he staged a one-man boycott of whatever product or service was involved as a result of suffering. Hence he wore undyed cloth for most of his life because dyes were derived from indigo and other plants produced by slave labor in the West Indies.

There are some rather clear indications from Woolman's *Journal* that he got that way in part, at least, because of some unresolved feelings toward his parents. He reports that at about the age of nine he had a dream in which the sun caused a tree that had been "planted" by the moon to wither and die, after which "there appeared a being small of size full of strength and resolution moving swift from the north southward called a sun worm. Though I was a child this dream was instructive to me." [19] He doesn't tell us what the "instruction" was, but goes on to relate the following incident in which he killed with a stone a mother robin who had three babies. He reports then, "However pleased with the exploit, I was shortly seized with horror and remorse, as having killed an innocent creature while she was careful for her young." [20] He then killed the young ones also to spare them suffering, and tells how the thought of his destructive act haunted him. "I mention this," he continues, "to show how God the parent of all creatures hath placed that in the human mind which doth instruct and incite to exercise goodness toward all His creatures." [21] Finally, he recounts an incident which he says occurred when he was about twelve years old in which he "made an undutiful reply" to a reproof given him by his mother. Later, when his father learned of the incident, he rebuked Woolman, who then tells us, "I knew myself greatly to blame, and in shame and confusion remained silent." [22]

The dream is rather clearly built around the oedipal theme in which the "sun" (father) attacks the "moon" (mother) but from which conflict emerges the "sun worm" (John) "small of size full of strength and resolution." The two following incidents show John's discomfort with his aggressiveness shown in the dream. Many small boys kill birds and "talk back" to their mothers, but this one's feelings toward his parents made these incidents very painful and instructive, or so the juxtaposition of the accounts strongly suggests. His fear of the aggressiveness (probably originally directed toward his father, though this is not clear) appears to have given him an unusual sensitivity to aggressive acts, both in himself and later on toward others. His sense of shame mentioned on the occasion of his father's rebuke later developed into a shame tolerance great enough to run the risk of appearing "odd" to his contemporaries. That is, his conscious awareness of it as a child made it possible to develop a tolerance for it later. He had no tolerance for guilt and did everything he could to avoid it. This pattern of shame tolerance and guilt avoidance is typical of saints in Western culture, where most persons have probably been better able to tolerate guilt than shame, and had rather be found a knave than a fool.

My point in presenting this rather extended digression about Woolman is not that he was "sick" (if he was, it is a kind of sickness that we should try to cultivate), but to show some of the roots of his greatness in what was for him originally coping behavior in his struggle to maintain his identity and worth as a boy. His theological outlook and strong religious faith undergirded and reinforced this dynamic, but not every Quaker who shared his faith shared his great sensitivity and compassion.

There remained until nearly the end of his life some "bound" aspects of his comportment which suggest that the residuals of childhood continued to exercise some maintenance control. After a dream in which he saw oppressed persons working in a mine, he determined not to use silver vessels to eat and drink from as he "saw that people getting silver vessels to set off their tables at entertainments was often stained with worldly glory." [23] Soon afterward, while dining with a friend he refused to drink from a silver cup, and asked to be brought drink in something else. This action, which could only have the effect of putting someone out slightly, appears to have been motivated as much by his desire to escape the taint of worldliness as by wishing to "demonstrate" on behalf of oppressed silver miners.

But the whole pattern of his life was not thus bound to the childhood needs in which it originated. It was, rather, directed toward calling attention to real and terrible evils in his society, and was very effective in that according to the testimony of those who knew him. Because of Woolman, slaveholding among the Quakers in America diminished, though to what degree we cannot determine, and the longer-range impact is difficult to measure. But we know that his lonely stand came to be shared by millions within one generation of his death in 1772. His participation was salvatory. [24]

Other persons who might well be functioning at this level include the group called "self-actualizing people" by Abraham Maslow. First described in his book *Motivation and Personality* in 1954, this concept was a continuing focus of his attention until his death. [25] Maslow characterized self-actualizers as able to perceive reality efficiently and be comfortable with it; to accept others, and nature; as spontaneous; as focused on problems other than themselves; as relatively detached; as autonomous of culture and environment; as having a continued freshness of appreciation; as capable of experiencing the "oceanic feeling"; as having a strong "fellow feeling" for mankind; as being capable of deep interpersonal relations; as possessing a democratic (as opposed to authoritarian) character structure; as able to discriminate between means and ends; as possessing a philosophical, unhostile sense of humor; as being creative; and as resisting enculturation. He also noted some imperfections such as vanity, ruthlessness, and a certain disregard for the needs of others.[26]

This description could well fit a person able to live mainly at the participatory level, though as we can see from the imperfections mentioned that he might not actually do it. One factor here is that Maslow's self-actualizers were all college students still in the process of development, which inevitably affects the quality of participation. Maslow's conception of self-actualization as being possible only after certain basic needs are met is quite compatible with the position which I have taken in this book, though I think that some of the needs he discusses are not so basic as he does.[27]

At this level the factor of personal choice comes to play a very prominent role in behavior. Level Five people *are able* to participate in the salvatory process, but they may not always choose to do so. They may perceive rightly at times that full participation will endanger their health and even their lives, and make a decision to remain detached. At this level the role of values becomes quite important, as Maslow noted with his self-actualizers. The choices made by Level Five persons will reflect rather directly the values they profess to hold. The emphasis in Christianity on sacrificial self-giving will make a real difference in Christians living at this level, while at lower levels the role of theology is not so directly decisive in behavior, serving more as a justification for it than a guide. In Level Four it begins to play a significant role, but is less of an actual determinant before that. At lower levels stated values serve more a purpose of giving the individual a sense of sharing a common set of ideals with others, reassuring him, and raising his identity and worth quotient.

Level Six. Here we find persons participating almost entirely for the sake of the participation itself and its ramifications. It seems to me that Jesus probably reached this level toward the end of his ministry, though there are indications that he was not without maintenance problems earlier (e.g., the story of the Syrophoenician woman in Mark 7:24–30 suggests that he shared the prejudices common to his people, but also that he was developing beyond them). Francis of Assisi certainly looked like a Level Six person to his contemporaries.

Recently, David C. Duncombe has presented a description of the mature Christian, using categories based on personality testing in his *The Shape of the Christian Life*.[28] While I must take issue with Duncombe's "sheep and goats" classification, in which those who meet his criteria are called Christians and those who fail are not (though he acknowledges that there are "degrees" of Christian maturity), I can commend his five criteria. They are: (*a*) a freeing sense of security, (*b*) self-knowledge, (*c*) accurate perception, (*d*) honest expression, and (*e*) adequate response.[29] He holds the first to be basic, though acknowledges that it has less empirical basis in personality test results.[30] His descriptions of persons exemplifying these qualities are detailed and will prove helpful to ministers, for whom the book is written, in identifying persons who may be living at Levels Five and Six.[31] Caution should be observed when using such an approach embodying ideals of perfection not to relegate everyone who misses these marks into the "goat" category, however, and to repeat the errors of pietisms of the past. Few will be seen as meeting all of them, but it is hoped that the dynamic scale being presented in this chapter can show the relative possibilities in anyone without falling into "sheep and goats" thinking.

Even if one is functioning at this level of maximal potential for salvatory participation, there is no certainty that this participation will become actual. During my boyhood in Tennessee the names to conjure with were Robert E. Lee and Thomas J. "Stonewall" Jackson, the Civil War generals. These were the models of "Christian gentlemen" that boys and young men were urged to emulate. Though Jackson's credentials as a military tactician place him almost in a class by himself, it is doubtful that in our modern view of human functioning he would serve as an all-around model. He was moody and a rigid disciplinarian who could not tolerate the sight of wounded soldiers.

With Lee the situation is otherwise. He seems to have been a man who would have stood out as a superior human being in any age. In a recent study entitled "The Southern Soldier Saint," Samuel Southard has pointed out that Lee especially fulfilled the ideals of the postwar South that had to control its tendency toward violence and the need for revenge. These ideals were "identity and definiteness, fidelity and steadfastness, self-restraint and serenity." [32] Southard quotes a federal general who knew Lee at West Point as saying of him that "all his accomplishments and alluring virtues appeared natural in him, and he was free from anxiety, distrust and awkwardness that attend a sense of inferiority." [33] This certainly reads like the description of a Level Six person, free from identity and worth needs, able fully to participate. All the more striking because of his youth (Level Six patterns are rare among young persons, as noted in our discussion of Level Four), this description seemed to have fitted him accurately all his adult life. The one serious question that Southard raised about Lee's character was his refusal to take positions on complicated public questions, whether political or ecclesiastical.[34] It could be argued that this was deliberate on his part, however, and resulted from his judgment that his function as a model, already established in his lifetime, precluded his taking stands on matters that were not of the utmost gravity.

In spite of all this great potential, it is probably true that Lee's total contribution and pattern of participation was on balance destructive. His choice to remain loyal to the State of Virginia rather than to the United States meant that his great leadership capacity and considerable military skill enabled the Confederacy to hold out much longer than would probably have been the case otherwise.[35] This prolongation of the war meant leaving the South desolate and embittered and the North vindictive and determined to prevent a new rising of the South for decades to come.

Why did Lee make such a choice? He stated in a letter to his son, "As an American citizen I prize the Union very highly and know of no personal sacrifice I would not make to preserve it, save that of honor." [36] Southard notes rightly that to Lee "honor" essentially meant loyalty to his family and peers of the Virginia aristocracy. It had both an "identity and worth" aspect, and in this respect represented a regression to Level Three, but also a value dimension, in which Lee, accurately surveying his options, chose in the light of the values he had inherited. This was in conflict with his personal opposition to slavery, and powerful enough to override it. We cannot know which of these elements was predominant, but we do know that on no other occasion in his career did his behavior so strongly suggest compensatory maintenance, which is an indication that the value dimension was the more important, and that he made an essentially free choice.

My point here, of course, is to try to demonstrate in the life of a well-known historical figure the ambiguity of life even at the highest levels of the salvation-health relationship. One may wish to argue that the ultimate good done by Lee outweighed the evil, since he doubtless did mitigate the antipathy between North and South to some extent after the war. Yet even if this were somehow weighed as greater, the destructive effects on thousands of lives and the fiber of the nation of that awesome decision cannot be denied. Once again, we see that what Duncombe has called "adequate response" depends not only upon health, which provides the basic potential, but also upon the total grasp of the situation and the values that guide decisions. And finally, we see that at this level no response is going to be adequate in every respect, for the range of choice is too great and the "mutually obstructive" consequences incalculable. Life is shot through with tragedy at its peak levels as well as those where bare maintenance is the rule.

Before an attempt is made to bring together in a summary schematic diagram the diverse materials of this model, there is one question to which some attention must be given. Is such a model as this really helpful in attempting to understand actual persons who may be functioning at different levels in different aspects of their lives? Is it not possible to have a Level Five vocational pattern and a Level Three marriage, for instance? What of teen-agers who do very well academically but are withdrawn socially? While recognizing that persons certainly do function in apparently different ways in different areas of their lives, I would hold that these nevertheless will constitute a pattern when they are understood in dynamic relationship to one another. The progressive and able professional man who seems to use the church for purely maintenance purposes may often be found to be also using his job for maintenance purposes—but there a compensatory development provides the maintenance, whereas the church is strictly a holding operation. Only exhaustive analysis of many cases could begin to demonstrate that this is true, so I can only invite the reader to test it in his own experience.

The schematic diagram shown on page 116 is intended to assist the reader in understanding the essential features of the model that has been discussed more clearly than may have been possible in the discursive presentation. The letters M, D, and P represent maintenance, development, and participation, respectively. The numbers 1 to 6 ascending the page from left to right represent the levels of the salvation-health relational potential. The lines between the letters and the numbers show the principal energy corridors and their direction of flow. In order to keep the schematization from being overly complicated, relatively minor flows have not been depicted, with the exception of the participatory interaction at Level One, which though relatively slight is of great importance. There the

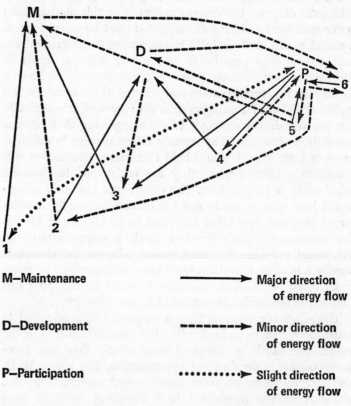

SCHEMATIC REPRESENTATION
OF SALVATION–HEALTH MODEL

M–Maintenance   ⎯⎯⎯⎯→ Major direction
                                              of energy flow

D–Development   – – – – → Minor direction
                                              of energy flow

P–Participation   •••••••• → Slight direction
                                              of energy flow

dotted line with an arrow at both ends indicates that persons living at Level One both give and receive in some degree, however small. The solid lines indicate a major direction of energy flow, while the dashed lines indicate relatively minor directions.

Thus at Level One we see the massive flow toward maintenance, with no developmental involvement and little participation. At Level Two we find a focus on development represented by the solid line, with maintenance and development playing lesser roles, and so on. Finally, at Level Six we find participation to be the principal direction of flow, with maintenance and development playing supporting roles, along with feedback from participation itself.

NOTES

1. Cf. n. 46, Chapter III, above. The technical term that von Bertalanffy has employed to designate this tendency is *equifinality*, suggesting that organisms develop toward the same "end" though often by different routes (*General System Theory: Essays on Its Foundation and Development*, pp. 132–134; George Braziller, 1969).

2. *Ibid.*, p. 160.

3. Alfred, Lord Tennyson, "Ulysses," in Paul R. Lieder, Robert M. Lovett, and Robert K. Root, *British Poetry and Prose* (Houghton Mifflin Company, 1938), Vol. II, pp. 517–518. The lines referred to are as follows, placed in the mouth of Ulysses after he finally reached home from the Trojan War:

> 'Tis not too late to seek a newer world.
> Push off, and sitting well in order smite
> The sounding furrows; for my purpose holds
> To sail beyond the sunset, and the baths
> Of all the western stars, until I die.
> It may be that the gulfs will wash us down:
> It may be we shall touch the Happy Isles,
> And see the great Achilles, whom we knew.
> Tho' much is taken, much abides; and tho'
> We are not now that strength which in old days
> Moved earth and heaven; that which we are, we are;
> One equal temper of heroic hearts,
> Made weak by time and fate, but strong in will
> To strive, to seek, to find, and not to yield.

Gordon W. Allport in his idea of propriate striving has developed a similar theme within the context of his personality theory (*Becoming: Basic Considerations for a Psychology of Personality*, pp. 47–51; Yale University Press, 1955).

4. Above, pp. 54 f.

5. Above, pp. 84 ff.

6. Other candidates for the *sine qua non* of personality functioning are security, love, and acceptance. Although all of them are quite important for some individuals, none is pervasive enough to give it universal status. Security, which was made relatively popular by the great psychiatrist Harry Stack Sullivan, refers to the inner quiescence of the organism. Sullivan regarded the absence of anxiety as the primary signal of mental health, and hence security, or the absence of anxiety, was seen as fundamental. Others have held that some anxiety is present and even quite appropriate at some times, however, such as at the beginning of a difficult performance. "Creative insecurity" is more than a nice phrase, but points to a genuine condition for novel participation.

Love and acceptance are very important for the maintenance of most persons (hermits appear to be an exception), though I would hold that they are important precisely because they confer and enhance identity and worth.

Having said this, I must also recognize that in dealing with maintenance dynamics in terms of identity and worth I am simplifying the complexities of motivation in individual cases, each of which has its unique features. Nevertheless, I believe that a grasp of the role played by identity and worth factors will lead to a basic understanding of any case.

7. Cf. above, pp. 69–70, 84. Erikson's conception of integrity vs. despair as characteristic of old age is discussed, *inter alia*, in *Childhood and Society* (W. W. Norton & Company, Inc., 1950), pp. 231–233.

8. Fear of losing one's identity is not the only factor in ritual, of course. Others are related to communal feelings, and in the case of religious practices, to the need for protection against the powerful experience of the divine—that is, to the need for an appropriate experience that does not overpower the worshiper.

9. I have discussed the conception of *transpropriate willing* in

some detail in *The Concept of Willing* (Abingdon Press, 1967), pp. 195–206. I regard this conception as a more accurate way of speaking about the human response to God's lure into further development and participation than Allport's notion of *propriate* striving (cf. n. 3, above), since it points to the necessity of risking the loss of selfhood, understood generically as the conservator of the identity of the past.

10. In presenting participation as the normative concept in this model, I realize that I am making the communal and collective life of man and God the ultimate goal. This will be disturbing to some readers steeped in our ultraindividualistic tradition. However, I must point out that in order to participate fully in the salvatory process, a person must at the same time be realizing his own "subjective aim," or to put it more familiarly, his own potential. Hence the individual and the collective are not finally at odds, though the reality of evil does bring them into conflict at points.

11. R. D. Laing, *The Politics of Experience* (Ballantine Books, Inc., 1967), pp. 146–168 *et passim*.

12. Kevin P. Phillips, *The Emerging Republican Majority* (Arlington House, Publishers, 1969).

13. See Karl A. Menninger, Paul W. Pruyser, Martin Mayman, *The Vital Balance: The Life Process in Mental Health and Illness* (The Viking Press, 1963), Chs. VIII, IX, for a comprehensive discussion of high-cost coping devices.

14. See Anna Freud, *The Ego and the Mechanisms of Defense* (International Universities Press, Inc., 1946), for the classical presentation of ego defenses. These include repression, regression, reaction formation, denial, projection, identification, intellectualization, compensation, isolation, undoing, and sublimation. Since her work appeared some of these conceptions have been considerably modified, and the term "compensation" as used in this present work is very much broader than the way she employed it.

15. Rubin and Gertrude Blanck, *Marriage and Personal Development* (Columbia University Press, 1968), p. 18.

16. John F. Cuber with Peggy B. Harroff, *The Significant Americans: A Study of Sexual Behavior Among the Affluent* (Appleton-Century-Crofts, 1965), Chs. 6 and 7.

17. Gordon W. Allport, *Pattern and Growth in Personality* (Holt, Rinehart and Winston, Inc., 1961), pp. 229–253.

18. The stages cited were developed by Laurence Kohlberg and his associates. Beginning with his doctoral dissertation, entitled "The Development of Modes of Moral Thinking and Choice in the Years Ten to Sixteen" (unpublished dissertation, University of Chicago, 1958), Kohlberg has continued to pursue research in this field since joining the faculty at Harvard. In an interview by Israel Shenker of *The New York Times* (Feb. 15, 1970), Kohlberg stressed the universal, transcultural character of these stages. Other prominent theories similar to this one are proposed by Robert F. Peck and Robert J. Havighurst, *The Psychology of Character Development* (John Wiley & Sons, Inc., 1960), and by Jean Piaget, *The Moral Judgment of the Child* (The Macmillan Company, 1955). Of these, Piaget's position stressed cognitive factors more and minimized somewhat the development of the affective life. All are solidly based on empirical research, and all emphasize the necessity of increasingly sophisticated socialization in order for the moral dimension to develop.

19. *The Journal of John Woolman,* ed. by Janet Whitney (Henry Regnery Company, 1950), pp. 2–3. Other editions of Woolman's *Journal* that I have seen omit the account of this dream, probably as being unworthy of him.

20. *Ibid.,* p. 3.

21. *Ibid.*

22. *Ibid.,* p. 4.

23. *Ibid.,* p. 194.

24. Some students of Woolman have argued that his relationship to his wife left much to be desired, since he was continually leaving home to attend to his mission, and was often gone for long periods of time, including his last journey to England, where he died. Yet there is much evidence that he cared for his wife, and he always left her well provided for (he was a highly successful tailor before beginning his second career as an advocate of emancipation; also, long absences between husband and wife were not uncommon in the eighteenth century).

25. Abraham Maslow, *Motivation and Personality* (Harper & Brothers, 1954).

26. *Ibid.*, pp. 203–229.
27. *Ibid.*, p. 201. Cf. also n. 6, p. 118, above.
28. David C. Duncombe, *The Shape of the Christian Life* (Abingdon Press, 1969), p. 18.
29. *Ibid.*, p. 23.
30. *Ibid.*, p. 187.
31. The persons who formed the testing population with which Duncombe worked were mostly college students, and hence were not themselves necessarily all living at these levels. There is no way to know whether even one individual was, since each of the tests used was focused upon only one of the five characteristics. That is, an individual might well have developed one capacity without the others, though theoretically they tend to go together.
32. Samuel Southard, "The Southern Soldier Saint," *Journal for the Scientific Study of Religion*, Vol. VIII, No. 1 (Spring, 1969), p. 41.
33. *Ibid.*
34. *Ibid.*, p. 42.
35. This is, of course, debatable, and has been debated hotly for over a century, but the fact remains that Lee and his lieutenants repeatedly beat the best the Union had to offer (or thought it had), while the Confederacy never won a major battle in the West, where its generals were of lower caliber.
36. Southard, "The Southern Soldier Saint," p. 43.

Chapter V

Implications of the Model
for Theological Anthropology

In Chapter III, I discussed at some length the general implications of process theology for a doctrine of salvation, and in that connection treated also in a general way its implications for anthropology. Here I shall attempt both to sharpen up these implications and to add to them specific points implied by the dynamic process model.

1. Genuine Ambiguity and Genuine Possibility

First I note that the model sharpens up considerably our understanding of man's essential ambiguity and possibility. That is, on the basis of this model we can affirm that both the traditional antagonists—Calvinists and Arminians—were generally right in their central conviction but wrong in denying the positions of each other. We can clearly see the ambiguity of life both as a result of the ecology of evil and the individual's own maintenance needs operating at all levels of the salvation-health model except the sixth. These are a part of man's *essential* situation, and will remain so as long as man is man.[1] But we can also clearly see that life lived on a level with sufficient health to provide a basis for full salvatory participation is more than a vague ideal. It is an actuality for some, and a possibility for many more—though not for all, due to the power of maintenance needs and hostile environments.

It is equally clear that this model has some rather radical implications for traditional understandings of man in Protestantism. That is, it enables us to affirm the central contentions of both the Calvinist and Arminian positions, but in a shape that neither could quite understand or accept. Let us look first at two implications of this view of ambiguity.

2. Healing Must Be Continual

In one sense this implication is not so strange to the tradition I have suggested. All streams in the tradition have stressed in one way or another that man is in need of continual forgiveness and grace, and that he does not "make it" to a peak of sanctity where these are no longer necessary.[2] But to think of this as *healing* in a literal sense is strange. Yet we note that from the moment of birth man is striving to maintain himself in an environment that is ambiguous at best and hostile at worst. He needs continual "repair" for development to take place. Even when he reaches levels on the salvation-health continuum where he is capable of participating quite fully in the salvatory process, he is still often in need of healing. To be sure, by then he may well be capable of healing himself in most instances. Challenges to his identity and worth, like cut fingers and bruises, can be recognized for what they are and dealt with.

In saying this I am asserting on the one hand the classical liberal position of the continuity between creation and redemption, and viewing them as perspectives on the health-salvation relationship. But I am asserting a much more radical need for healing (redemption) than the liberals allowed. They generally held that life might be lived in a continuous upward curve, with few dips or failings. I hold that the dips, as they are very much a part of the whole, and that compensation, and some of it very costly, are parts of every life; and that sin, the intentionality of evil, is pervasive in the lives of most.

3. Justification, Faith, and Forgiveness

These three central motifs of the Reformation are being treated together because of their intrinsic relationships, and because the effect of the dynamic process model is to make them regulatory rather than constituent principles of Christian life. We have already noted that salvation is viewed here primarily as the enhancement and preservation of personhood. It is not escape from divine punishment, because God is not concerned about punishment. That is a human invention, stemming from the childhood of the race.[3] Without a doctrine of divine punishment, the centrality of justification must finally be given up. Justification refers to the need for vindication against accusation of offense against the law. Without punishment the need for such vindication disappears.

Why, then, it may be asked, has the doctrine of justification persisted, even though divine punishment has not been emphasized except in very conservative circles for many years? The answer can be seen in the salvation-health model. Justification is a subjective need related to the basic worth factor in personality maintenance. It is particularly evident in Levels Three and Four, and in fact related directly to Luther's vocational situation in its classical formulation within Protestantism. However, it is not the central question in the Christian life, for some Christians (and non-Christians) develop to the point of no longer needing to ask it of themselves. This is, in fact, one meaning of participation for the sake of participation —one has moved beyond the necessity of participating in order to be justified.

If one need not be justified, in the ontological sense, then it is apparent that *faith* no longer has a function as the mode of justification in that sense. For Luther, justification by grace through faith was a genuinely sound and viable solution to an otherwise insoluble problem, that of escaping the divine wrath and having peace with God the Father. But for us who do not fear this wrath (whether we have a process theological outlook or not), it is not needed for this purpose. Nevertheless, it does have an important function as a vision of the past and present and future, which maximizes salvatory participation. At certain stages of development, notably those associated with Level Four, faith is also needed for the senses of identity and worth to be firm, even though these are not clearly recognized by other persons. So in that sense "justification" by faith continues to have a significant, if not final, function in the life of the Christian. This is not merely a belief in oneself and one's powers, but a commitment to participation based on a vision of reality which makes such participation meaningfully salvatory.

This kind of "justification" by faith also plays a role in other levels. At Level Three it may be a part of the maintenance syndrome and represent a rigidity of theological outlook. At Levels Five and Six it plays a regulatory role in times of stress, furnishing reassurance in the face of challenges to integrity, enabling one to engage in salvatory, though costly, participation and relationships. In this role it is more than a long-range vision by which one is lured into God's future; it is a personal "graspedness" undergirding the process of transpropriate willing.

Much of this is certainly not brand-new as an understanding of the nature and function of faith. What is new, I think, is the removal of the "all or nothing" character of faith. It is not something that one either has or does not have enough of to be saved, but rather one dimension of life that plays a role in the total salvatory process. In other words, this view of faith removes the obsessional quality which has been the plague of Protestantism, just as obsession about good works has been the plague of Catholicism. It does not mean, however, that a salvation by "works" theory is being advocated, as that has been traditionally understood. I shall return to this point in the next section.[4]

Forgiveness is a more complicated matter. Technically it

means to "let go" of the hold one has on a person because of a debt or offense of some kind. Elsewhere I have argued that this root meaning is often lost sight of in modern discussions of forgiveness and is essential for a proper understanding.[5] Forgiveness also means, of course, the shift in personal relationships from alienation to reconciliation, and this is what is usually in focus in discussions of it. Here we come to one of the most far-reaching implications of process theology. God does not have the kind of alienated hold on man that release through forgiveness implies.[6] He is not punitive in his attitude or legalistic. These are approaches to controlling behavior, as we have noted, that are characteristic of late childhood, though many persons do not develop further. They have been projected onto the deity by primitive man.

The other, more modern, meaning of forgiveness (which is in focus at some points in the Bible, notably in the story of the prodigal son) is that of overcoming personal estrangement. Though the concept and feeling of legal obligation is not entirely absent, the emphasis is upon the personal isolation and pain of alienation which is overcome by forgiveness, rather than upon a debt canceled. In this sense, forgiveness retains its status as a fundamental principle of the man-God relationship. It is needed whenever estrangement has come to characterize a man's stance and relationship to God, whether through indifference, hostility, or ignorance. This aspect of forgiveness is usually designated by the term "acceptance."[7]

So far we have been speaking of forgiveness purely in terms of the process conception of the God-man relationship. When we look at the model of the salvation-health relationship, we see that, although this discussion is probably on the right track as far as it goes, it does not go far enough to give us an adequate picture of the role of forgiveness in human life, which must of necessity have additional consequences for theological anthropology. In essence we find that forgiveness in the full sense of the word—encompassing both release from debt and the removal of the barriers to reconciliation—is a necessity for man.

This is so because man does not come into the world fully developed and fully participating. As a part of his development he necessarily passes through stages in which he views life in terms of "power and punishment" and "law and order" as we have noted in the previous chapter. In these stages both aspects of forgiveness become crucial for continued development. Not only does a young person need to experience the forgiveness of others, and in particular his parents (in "nuclear family" cultures such as ours),[8] but he first and foremost needs to experience the forgiveness of himself. Though this can best be seen in typical cases of an obviously depressed person being battered by a harsh and punitive superego, or primitive conscience, which overwhelms him with too many "shoulds" and "should nots," it is also present, though less obviously, in other persons whose development continues to progress.[9] Even in the generation coming of age, in which little overt evidence of guilt is to be noted, and who steadfastly insist that parents need their forgiveness (an important dynamic factor even in previous generations which usually has gone unacknowledged), there is a need for young persons to forgive themselves. Often they feel a sense of failure and alienation because they have not been able to achieve all they feel they might, or have not mended all the brokenness of the world. As Henry T. Close has pointed out, forgiveness is a condition and prelude to responsible action, not blame.[10] This applies as much to "emancipated" young people who cannot forgive themselves for failure and who then experience shame and alienation, as to "old style" people troubled by guilt and fear of punishment.[11]

All this is a corollary of the point stated earlier that the need for healing is continuous and a "normal" part of life. It is especially needed in salvation-health Level Two, where progressive development depends in no small measure upon the quality of forgiveness available. Healing depends upon forgiveness, in both its debt-releasing and alienation-overcoming dimensions in areas of life that reach far beyond the obviously psychological, as those who deal with psychosomatic problems well know. It makes firm the tottering identity and restores the sense of worth. Even in the upper levels of the continuum it is often needed, though there less continuously as the core maintenance factors become more stable. In times of personal and social crisis when choices are usually pregnant with consequences, those who turn out destructively make forgiveness a necessity for the chooser, no matter what his level, if he is to continue in his ability to participate in the salvatory process.

In all these situations the acceptance of God, which is always available, must be conveyed through a human relationship or relationships, except in those far advanced on the salvation-health continuum, who may be able to do their own mediating. For so deep a part of the human heritage is the need for absolute justification and absolution, and so remote seem the possibilities of attaining it that we cannot yet recognize that God does not hold us to an absolute standard. Rather, he participates in our lives by influencing our goals and behavior as one component of the reality of the world (cf. Chapter III, 2, above). This means that he fully sees the ambiguity and muddledness of our lives and does not hold out a stick for us to jump over at increasingly higher levels. Rather, he seeks to call and to lure us into the maximizing of beauty in our lives and the lives of all insofar as we can, recognizing that there may be many ways of doing this, and none free from the production of evil. He always accepts, though there are no debts to be forgiven. Yet he is in and with us in our struggles to find forgiveness, seeing that we must have it to meet the burdensome legacy of the past, and does not condemn us for needing it. He moves toward his own perfection through our "imperfections," finding amid them the beauty for his own life.

4. Sanctification

Traditionally, Protestants have been accustomed to think of sanctification as a purification process following upon justification. This conception has been under attack for some time, notably by Karl Barth,[12] so I have no claim to uniqueness in asserting that it is a less than adequate view of sanctification. We have already noted that justification is not needed as a description of a fundamental aspect of the man-God relationship, though it remains as a regulatory principle, or subsidiary aspect. Hence whatever sanctification is, it is not to be understood principally as a process following justification. Nor is it to be understood primarily in terms of purification, though aspects of it may at times be so understood.

What, then, is it? From the point of view of the model presented in the previous chapter, it must be seen primarily in terms of fulfillment of potential for participation in the salvatory process, which is much greater in the last two levels in the model, though not entirely absent in any. It is, indeed, processive in character, and its fundamental characteristic is the ability to envision a transpropriate future and to act upon it—to will transpropriately.[13] This ability is generally found at Levels Five and Six, but as we have seen in the case of Robert E. Lee, it is not guaranteed there. Nor is it necessarily lacking at lower levels, even Level One. The person seemingly hopelessly ensnarled in a psychotic or addictive situation in which he can barely maintain himself often with appropriate help finds the courage to envision a life free from such entrapment and to act upon it. He is willing transpropriately, and genuinely participating in the salvatory process, which is sanctification.

Is membership in the Christian community and belief in the Christian tradition necessary for such sanctification? If we mean by Christian community the institutional church, the answer must certainly be no. But the influence of Jesus and his "input" into the historical process far exceeds the boundaries of the church, or any other institution or culture. In our culture it is pervasively, if ambiguously, represented. Hence sanctification is where we find it: in the ghetto, in the town and suburbs, even in the churches and the government! As we have noted, Christian faith does seem to be an important element in the development of the ability to live life at Levels Five and Six. But it is not a necessary one, and certainly Christian belief may be used as a crutch for maintenance purposes as well as an inspiration to transpropriate behavior, depending upon *how* it is held.

Sanctification, then, is centrally a matter of finding one's vocation in life and striving to fulfill it. But "vocation" must not be understood too narrowly as occupation alone. One's vocation may have several dimensions that are not even apparently related. Their unity may not even be grasped by the person whose vocation it is, and some more conspicuous dimensions may be primarily compensatory. Yet underneath, where there is a significant degree of participation in the salvatory process, there will be seen upon careful examination to be a unity. This unity will be characterized by an increased capacity for love in all its forms, including self-love, sexual love, and love that gives to others sacrificially. As Daniel Day Williams has cogently argued, these forms of love are not opposed to one another but are organically related.[14] Purity still may play a significant role in this process, but it is not to be sought for itself as it has been in the past (though this was a perversion of even the Puritan tradition), and is not to be equated automatically with abstinence from any kind of activity, however necessary this may be for some.

To summarize, sanctification has been described as fundamentally a process of fulfillment of potential for participation in the salvatory process. It may be found to some extent on all salvation-health levels, and wherever it is found its distinguishing mark is transpropriate willing, the ability to act beyond one's known and familiar self. At higher levels this capacity is still present but may be less in evidence, since the self has been expanded to include many kinds of appropriate action. There the capacity to love in all its forms, as well as to act transpropriately when the situation calls it forth, becomes increasingly relevant.

This position is not a salvation "by works" understanding

of sanctification because in no sense are the loving and willing discussed above attempts to "buy" God's favor, which is at the root of traditional works-righteousness theologies. God's favor does not need to be bought; man has that. What he needs is the power to know and to respond to the lure of God toward his future, and this comes through development. In this development God himself participates, not always decisively, as we noted before, but always present. Through the gospel of Jesus Christ which has flowed into history he participates in a uniquely powerful way, enabling those who have been significantly touched by it to put back into the salvatory process what they got from it, but better, because of their own unique contributions.[15]

5. The Social and Political Gospel

Here we run squarely into two rather opposite criticisms of process theology for which the model must provide some answer or else be found crucially lacking in relevance. The first of these is that in an essentially social conception of reality such as the one we are dealing with, the individual does not really exist anyway with any integrity. Consequently, the question of a social gospel is redundant, for there is no individual gospel; only a salvation by participation in which the identity of the individual is ultimately lost. To press the point even further, the whole process understanding is not obviously compatible with any conception of individual identity which has a life of its *own*, with all its stress upon relationship and interconnectedness.

Paul A. Mickey has dealt helpfully with this point by contending that man as an individual can be understood within a process framework as exemplifying *"relative autonomy, developmentalism, dynamic relation of conscious and unconscious processes,* and *affect or feeling."* [16] In making this assertion, Mickey has availed himself also of the work of David Rapaport, the late psychologist who made significant contributions to ego psychology, which of course means that he worked along lines close to those represented in this book. I believe that he has essentially and effectively answered the question of the integrity of the individual within process thought, as well as the question of the presumably change-less "soul" or "self" in a changing body, to which his essay was primarily addressed. The individual is relatively autonomous from his relationships and has his own center of conscious and unconscious life in dynamic relationship. It is he who develops, however much of this development is dependent upon, and in an "open system" relationship with, the environ-ment. The absence of the traditional changeless soul does not diminish this individuality, a relatively enduring center of feeling, acting, and thinking. The question of his survival be-yond the death of the physical organism has already been discussed (see p. 76, above), so I shall not pursue it here.

The second major criticism of process theology is, in effect, that it is too individualistic and is, in fact, analogous to the perfectionistic pietisms of the past in its emphasis upon the fulfillment of the subjective aim—spelled out in terms of lov-ing and willing in the hierarchical model. Does this not mean that only the healthy can be saved, and since most persons are not healthy, and probably cannot become so, are they not left out, to say nothing of the "structures" of society? At best, is it not a new version of the classical fundamentalist approach of saving the world through individual evangelism? That is, do we not have to wait until enough people are able to func-tion at the two top levels, with perhaps a sprinkling of young people at Level Four (compensatory development) in order to make any effective change in society?

In answering this question we must begin by noting once more that all persons can participate to some extent in the salvatory process, even though this will be severely limited in many instances. In the second place, we must note that even if a majority of persons in our society could somehow be enabled to participate in the salvatory process at Level Five or Six, we still would have no guarantee that society could be changed significantly.

This is so partly because it is in the nature of institutions to function primarily at the maintenance level, however compensated by growth and development. Institutions are not individuals capable of response to the lure of a future which might well dispense with them. They can and do change, of course. Sometimes this change is due primarily to buffeting by the environment, which may result in creative response or a tightening of the defenses. The tobacco industry in this country now exemplifies both responses at different levels, for instance. Faced with what appears to be an almost certain prohibition on the manufacture of cigarettes within the next decade or so, the major companies are fighting a defensive battle of attrition, using denial as the major defense, while at the same time quietly shifting their energies and capital into the production of goods that are not under fire. This appears to mean that only the farmers and warehousemen, who continue to believe in denial, will be left holding the bag. All these operations exemplify maintenance, but the shift is far more adaptive. It is true that institutions sometimes do move beyond the maintenance level when they have sufficient leadership functioning at Levels Five and Six. Unfortunately, most "charismatic" leaders are heavily compensated maintenance or development persons (though not all), which makes them able to communicate well with those whom they are leading, but considerably impairs their vision of where to lead.

Another reason that there can be no guarantees that institutional change will be salvatory is that even persons functioning at the top two levels respond to situations in terms of their values, which, as we pointed out in the case of Robert E. Lee, may lead them to choose courses of action which ultimately prove destructive. Although the Greek heroes in the Trojan War were not all necessarily so far up the salvation-health ladder, the theme of the *Iliad* and of all Greek tragedy is essentially that of the evil done unintentionally by men of goodwill and narrow values. This theme continues to be played out on the world stage even today.

What, then, can be done? If institutions are more or less intractable and the men who run them apt to be unreliable and shortsighted, must we not agree with Luther and consign the world to the devil, while seeking to save the beauty that flows from the lives of the few? My generation of intellectuals in its formative years gave essentially affirmative answers to this question. We did not see how the structures could be changed, so cowed were we by the holocaust of World War II and its aftermath—the Cold War, the bomb, and the will of the Truman and Eisenhower majorities for life in an unrocked boat which would somehow weather those perilous seas. It has taken the civil rights movement, the student revolt and black uprising, and finally the women's liberation movement to show us that life in an unrocked boat is as impossible for us as was a "return to normalcy" after World War I.

All this means that we must accept the risks of involvement with men and issues, whether or not we find them to be participation-oriented and clear-cut. Most of the men will, in fact, be maintenance-oriented and most of the issues cloudy. The more tightly the men cling to identity and worth, and the more fuzzy the issues, the greater the risks that attempting to move, lead, push, cajole, persuade, and manipulate them will lead into unforeseen (or if foreseen, minimized) difficulty. Nevertheless, the social structure must be changed so that full salvatory participation is a possibility for the many rather than the few, as it is today, even though some of the beauty that now exists must be risked.

To minimize these risks, those who have eyes to see and ears to hear must accept the responsibility of helping others toward higher levels of potential participation. It is not true, as has often been argued (mostly by those who feared their own self-awareness), that movement up the levels of the salvation-health continuum will produce less commitment and social concern. It does sometimes happen that in the course of psychotherapy or counseling a person comes to the realization that the basis, genetically, of his concern is a love-hate struggle with his family, and this may precipitate a recoil from his current value system. However, when this compensatory material is worked through, he will emerge with firmer and less rigidly held commitments, though the content may be somewhat altered. The danger here is, of course, that the compensatory elements will not be worked through, in which case the withdrawal from commitment may become relatively fixed.

Here it must be noted that the "transformation of consciousness" sought by the radical left can only be genuinely effective in persons who are functioning at Levels Five and Six, and to some extent at Level Four. In levels lower than these the "transformation of consciousness" can only mean the substitution of one set of rigidly held values for another, the familiar phenomenon of the reciprocity of authoritarianisms. Thus no matter how much heavily compensated persons endorse slogans containing the words "liberation," "awareness," "in touch with feelings," and the like, they remain essentially authority-oriented.[17]

Those who would seek to communicate with groups must recognize this aspect of the situation, and not be deceived into believing that rhetoric or even discussion has transformed more than the surface of consciousness. For clearly identified goals in which the risks are reasonably well understood, however, the attempt must still be made to mobilize persons at every level to change the oppressive character of some aspects of our society. It was worth the effort to arouse the conscience of legislators, for instance, when the white students and clergy converged on the South in the "Freedom Rides" of the early '60s, even though it was subsequently demonstrated that both blacks and whites remained prejudiced toward one another upon intimate personal contact.

All this is to say that we must proceed with the transformation of our society, and, by implication, of all societies with dimensions of oppression, by all the means at our disposal. But considerably more care needs to be exercised in choosing both goals and personnel than has been the case until now. I speak here primarily to the churches, but the same is true for those outside the church who seek permanent and salvatory change.

If, as I have suggested, the process currently is "pregnant" with possibilities of radical change, it is clear that we cannot predict with any degree of certainty what the direction of change will be. It may well be that the holocaust is indeed upon us, brought on by both turmoil from within and hostility from without. In such circumstances many will agree with Nobel Prize winner Albert Szent-Györgyi, who has published *his* anthropology entitled *The Crazy Ape*.[18] In an interview published in *The New York Times* (Feb. 20, 1970), he urged the young to give up, saying: "I would share with my classmates rejection of the whole world as it is—all of it. Is there any point in studying and work? Fornication—at least that is something good. What else is there to do? Fornicate and take drugs against this terrible strain of idiots who govern the world."

Many of us have shared this sentiment at least to some extent in recent days. But we cannot be sure that the pregnancy of our time will not be thus aborted by the incompetence of those in power. There are also signs of salvatory change in the midst of repression and violence. God calls those who can hear to participate in this change and to assume the risks. In spite of many contemporary improvements in obstetrical methods, birth continues to be a time of anxiety and terror as well as of joy and hope. We must live through the former to realize the latter. Thus process does not always signify smooth transition, but sometimes radical disjuncture, that what is truly salvatory from the past may be conserved and given new life.

NOTES

1. This position is obviously not totally congruent with traditional conceptions of the Fall of man, though it is not far from conceptions held by such theologians as Reinhold Niebuhr and Paul Tillich. Both described the Fall as inevitable if man is to be man with freedom, and ascribe to anxiety the key role in producing it, though Tillich took a more positive view, seeing the Fall as man's departure from "dreaming innocence" into actual existence. Yet both still held in some fashion to the idea that the Fall does not belong to man's essence. This is, of course, congruent with the story of the Fall in Gen., ch. 3, but in the case of Tillich, at least, it is due as much to fundamental loyalty to the idealistic tradition in philosophy which stretches back to Plato, who held that the existence of man is only a shadowy representation of essential reality.

I hold that a break with this tradition is justified on empirical grounds and to some extent on philosophical grounds. The empirical grounds are man's observed hostility and destructiveness, including his self-destructiveness, which he shares in part with the animal kingdom, but which in man goes beyond anything in nature, due to his superior cognitive ability. This evidence is not coercive, admittedly, as many intelligent men cling to the idea of man's essential goodness. Yet both clinically and politically, man's destructiveness is so massive in its manifestation that it cannot all be ascribed to the frustration and distortion of constructive aims. Or to put it more precisely, the frustration and distortion of such aims is an essential part of life, due to the pressure of the environment and man's long developmental climb, in which he experiences the frustration of both love and aggressive impulses, and the anxiety attendant upon them, both consciously and unconsciously.

This brings us to the philosophical grounds upon which I hold ambiguity to be an essential part of man's life. The mutual destructiveness of nature, as well as its development toward beauty, is shared by man, and when centered intentionally, is sin. As noted earlier in the text, sin is always a deflection from the sub-

jective aim of fulfillment, though it may lead to short-term satisfaction. Life involves genuine tragedy as well as sin, however.
Most of man's destructiveness is a combination of tragedy, in
which circumstances force choices that provide no really constructive options, and sin, in which anxiety and distorted vision
lead to choosing options that are even less constructive than
might be.

2. Holiness groups constitute an exception to this general rule.

3. Cf. the discussion of moral development on pp. 106–107, above.

4. Though the model has no direct implications for the larger
question of the relationship between faith and reason in theology,
it will be evident that I hold that there is no genuine conflict
between the two. Of the two, faith is prior in the sense that its
essence is to be grasped by the power of the Christian story
(presentational mode, see Foreword), but it can be clarified and
generalized through rational analysis (discursive mode), and
finally is indirectly subject in part to confirmation, refutation, or
modification in the light of empirical analysis (empirical mode).
The drawing of implications from the salvation-health model,
which includes an empirical dimension, is an example of this
latter operation. It speaks through the discursive mode to the
presentational mode, suggesting some modifications in our understanding of the Christian story.

5. James N. Lapsley, "Reconciliation, Forgiveness, Lost Con-
tracts," *Theology Today,* Vol. XXIII, No. 1 (April, 1966), pp.
44–59.

6. Although in his "primordial nature" God is ultimately the
creator of all the cosmos, he is the creator of individual men only
in part, since their lives derive in part from the physical prehensions of the past, and also in part from themselves in their
freedom. It remains true that God contributes to the subjective
aim of man, and that through sin man becomes alienated from
God, nevertheless it is not true that man "owes" complete conformity to God's will, since such conformity is an abstraction
from each actual occasion, and has no independent status apart
from the occasion. In other words, there is no implicit "contract"
between man and God, the violation of which gives rise to the
need for forgiveness in the technical sense. In this sense the
Biblical idea of a covenant between God and man has a more

limited applicability to the modern situation than many contemporary theologians have held. Its meaning as obligation is only partial, though its meaning as relationship for those in the Christian tradition is unimpaired.

7. Acceptance does sometimes connote an "in spite of" factor in the relationship, suggesting that the accepted party possesses an odious quality of some sort in the eyes of the accepting party. However, it does not necessarily have this connotation, and experience in counseling and psychotherapy strongly underlines the idea that acceptance must *not* be "in spite of" some such personally odious characteristic. There may well be some aspects of the counselee's behavior of which the counselor does not approve, but this does not mean that he finds the counselee personally odious. If this is a condition of human healing, should we expect that God will find man odious? Rather, divine acceptance is always available for men who can find in relationships that the odium which they feel about themselves has been projected onto God as his attitude toward them.

8. By the term "nuclear family" I mean a family constituted primarily of parents and their offsprings, even though other relatives may be living in the household as adjunct members of the family. In extended kinship systems, grandparents, aunts, uncles, and even cousins are an integral part of the family, whether they live under the same roof or not, and take an active part in child-rearing.

9. This is true even in persons whose character is so shaped that it has an antisocial impact on society as a whole, as in, for instance, the Mafia subculture, which develops very rigid character structures with strong superegos that adhere strictly to rules and exhibit intense loyalties. Only in genuinely truncated development in which parents and parent surrogates fail to impart personal standards of conduct do we find persons who are incapable of guilt or shame.

10. Henry T. Close, "Forgiveness and Responsibility: A Case Study," *Pastoral Psychology*, Vol. XXI, No. 205 (June, 1970), pp. 19–25.

11. Elsewhere I have argued that the shame-ridden cannot easily accept forgiveness from a counselor through confession, but this is a different matter from the need to forgive oneself ("Reflec-

tions on the Electric Circus," *Journal of Pastoral Care,* Vol.
XXIII, No. 1 [March, 1969], p. 13).

12. Karl Barth, *Church Dogmatics,* tr. and ed. by G. T. Thomson,
G. W. Bromiley, T. F. Torrance *et al.,* 4 vols. (Edinburgh: T. &
T. Clark, 1936–1960), IV, 2, pp. 500–502. Elsewhere, under
the topic of vocation and Christian liberty, Barth appears to allow for some kind of process in development of the Christian
life (*ibid.,* IV, 3, 2, pp. 664 ff.).

13. Here I wish to note the similarities and differences between my
position on the question of the will and that of Rollo May, whose
Love and Will (W. W. Norton & Company, Inc., 1969) con-
stitutes a major contribution to the subject. The similarities are
considerably more significant than the differences. May wishes
to demonstrate that we cannot get along without a viable conception of will, and in my opinion does so cogently. His central
contention is that *intentionality* (the act of tending toward or
against something or someone) is the core of the notion of will,
and that it is pervasive of human life (*Love and Will,* pp.
223 ff.). With this I certainly have no quarrel, and agree that
modern psychology in all its forms has greatly impoverished itself by attempting to ignore the will factor. Further, his contention that therapy, when successful, brings about a union of
conscious intention and unconscious intentionality I regard as a
fundamental way of understanding the therapeutic process (cf.
my discussion of this same point in "Willing and Selfhood," *The
Concept of Willing,* pp. 196–206; Abingdon Press, 1967).

I also agree that, when they are functioning without significant
distortion, love and will are very closely related, and that they
both derive from something like "care" as May contends, taking his cue from Heidegger (*Love and Will,* pp. 289 ff.). I
prefer to discuss this basic quality of life in terms of the drive
toward the fulfillment of the subjective aim, as has been noted.
But I agree that the splitting of love and will as being respectively derived from sexual and aggressive drives is a fundamental
error, and one that orthodox, dual-drive Freudians have often
fallen into. The *pathologies* of love and will polarize toward
these drives, but when they are functioning in an integrated person who is able to participate appropriately, this is not the case.
I believe the lasting contribution of May's work will be the
clear demonstration of this point through his case material.

On the other hand, there is a central point that May makes with which I cannot agree, and I believe it considerably weakens his work as a whole. This is his dismissal of dynamic psychological concepts, such as id, ego, and superego, as a "compartmentalization," which "is an important part of the reason why the problem of will has remained insoluble within the orthodox psychoanalytic tradition" (*ibid.*, p. 199). I do not believe that this is the case, and that the admitted insolubility of the will problem in the orthodox tradition is due rather to the dogged determinism of those persons, as in fact May has cogently pointed out (*ibid.*, pp. 196–198). His argument that the tripartite structural model of psychoanalysis represents a compartmentalization of the psyche similar to Descartes's "theory that the pineal gland, the organ at the base of the brain between body and head, was the place where the soul was located" (*ibid.*, p. 199) is a poor one. Rather, these "structures" are regarded as only relatively discrete functions which have no simple location in the body or the mind. Hence, May's contention that freedom developed in therapy, which is reflected in bodily movements and spontaneous acts, is a refutation of the ego psychology position that freedom inheres in the ego is simply a misunderstanding of what is meant by the term "ego." The ego is involved in the total life of the organism, not only in conscious cognition. May's contention that freedom "must be a quality of the total self—the thinking-feeling-choosing-acting organism"—is a description of ego functions. It is true that such freedom affects also aspects of the personality associated with the id (sex) and morality (superego), as May says, but this is because of a relatively greater power of the ego to influence these dimensions.

Now, all this would be little more than semantic squabble were it not that May has sacrificed considerable analytic explanatory power by his rejection of ego psychology in favor of phenomenology. As Don S. Browning has noted with penetration: "A phenomenologically derived ontology of the human is weak for the very reason that it is strong. It is strong because it avoids various kinds of reductionism—reductions to childhood and infantile origins, reductions to naturalistic and physicalistic causal origins, reductions to social determinisms, etc. But it is for this very reason that phenomenology is weak. It makes it impossible to chart out the causal configurations involving infantile, biological, physical, and social factors which at least influence (although not necessarily causally determine) various human phenomena" ("The Influence of Psychology on Theology," in William B. Oglesby, Jr. [ed.], *The New Shape of Pastoral Theology,* p. 129; Abingdon Press, 1969). Browning goes on to point out that Merleau-Ponty, now regarded by many as the most important of the phenomenologists, recognized this problem and rejected the dominance of phenomenology over psychology in his essay "Difficulties Involved in a Subordination of Psychology."

The price paid by May for his rejection of dynamic psychology (in theory only, for his practice reflected in his casework and other writings shows him to be a master of basic dynamic understanding) is just what we would expect from Browning's critique of phenomenology; his approach lacks analytic power in understanding the various modes of willing. Intentionality is indeed central, but in itself does not get us very far. May fails to see that the kind of willing he seeks to produce in therapy is radically different from the kind he finds going on in it. Though he sees that the process of therapy does mean movement from wish to will to decision, he does not see that the kinds of decision he is speaking about mean getting beyond the boundaries of the old self in a transpropriate act, which can be understood as due to the increased power of the ego. He does speak of "the capacities of the human being to transcend the concrete situation of the immediate self-oriented desire and to live in the dimensions of past and future, and in terms of the welfare of the persons and groups upon whom his own fulfillment intimately depends" (*Love and Will,* p. 268). But this passage shows how vague he must become in order to make this point, caught as he is with the baggage of an understanding of selfhood derived from phenomenology. For a further discussion, see my analysis of "self" in "Willing and Selfhood," *The Concept of Willing,* especially pp. 179–188.

14. Daniel Day Williams, *The Spirit and the Forms of Love* (Harper & Row, Publishers, Inc., 1968). This point is a fundamental one in the book, in opposition to Anders Nygren and others who have made a radical disjunction between *agapē* (sacrificial love) and all other forms, but see especially Chs. IX, XI, and XII. This does not include the distortions and perversions

of love—narcissism, sexual abuse, and masochism, but applies to all true forms comprehended by Williams' definition: "Love is an expression of spirit. It is spirit seeking the enjoyment of freedom in communion with the other" (*ibid.*, p. 3).

15. The grace of God is thus manifested in human history and its processes, instead of being a *donum super-additum* (super added grace), as has been traditionally taught in supernaturalist theologies. It is nonetheless real and gracious, however, for it represents the self-giving of God in leading us into the salvatory process.

16. Paul A. Mickey, "Toward a Theology of Individuality: A Theological Inquiry Based on the Work of Alfred North Whitehead and David Rapaport" (unpublished doctoral dissertation, Princeton Theological Seminary, 1970), p. 329. Mickey also dealt with the question of the individuality of God, a thorny one in process thought. In doing so, he rejected three principal ideas about God put forward by Whitehead and his followers: that God is the *creative advance* of the universe, that God is the chief exemplification of all metaphysical principles, and that God is beyond personality. I believe that Mickey is moving in the right direction in attributing personality to God, and that it is compatible with the basic principles of process thought, though he has not as yet provided us with definitive substitutes for the other two categories (*ibid.*, pp. 325 ff.).

17. I recently had occasion to attend a lecture given by one of the most prominent older writers who has inspired the "new left." The audience, made up predominantly of college and graduate students, cheered heartily at everything the speaker had to say, whether he urged liberation, excoriated the Establishment, or urged its destruction. Some of this was undoubtedly due to the power of the group, but much of it may be attributed to the authority with which this man has been invested by the anti-authoritarian youth.

18. Albert Szent-Györgyi, *The Crazy Ape* (Philosophical Library, Inc., 1970). Szent-Györgyi discovered vitamin C in 1937.

Chapter VI

Implications for Ministry

1. Professional Theology

We must now see what these considerations may mean for the practice of ministry, for it is mainly there that their usefulness can be proved. We have said that the theological anthropology of the past has been deficient in providing an understanding of man which is profound enough to encompass both the ambiguity and the possibility of man's life, and coherent enough to provide for the continuity of ministry in all its dimensions. In this chapter I shall try to show that the anthropology developed in this book is essentially adequate for this task.

We have spoken before about "professional theology," which refers to the fundamental principles that guide a minister's work. That this can really be one "bag" and not several disjunctive and mutually contradictory ones is the basic contention which I have been making throughout this book. This does not mean that ministers have no use for psychology in counseling, "kerygmatic" theology for preaching, or a knowledge of the principles of organization for administration. They will continue to need these and other tools of ministry. But these tools need to be related to a basic theory of what ministry is trying to accomplish, and the understanding of man and his relationships that this involves. How much of this basic understanding needs to be communicated to those for whom the minister is responsible depends upon many factors. For some lay persons a knowledge of these principles will be very helpful and even necessary, but for others, relatively meaningless. It is not necessary to know the formula for aspirin in order to get relief from a headache. So it is not necessary or helpful in all cases to communicate to those who need help in participating more fully in the salvatory process—the goal of all ministry, all of the theory upon which the help rests.

I say this again because of our inherited tendency to "preach" all of our theology in one way or another, and to dispel ideas of a hyperprofessional approach in which people are being manipulated without their knowledge. It is a prime responsibility of professional persons to know when it is appropriate to communicate what, and the unloading of one's whole "bag" when it is not wanted or needed is an irresponsible act. Manipulation is a dehumanizing act, but the protection from it must be the knowledge and responsibility of the professional person, not in his telling the parishioner everything he knows.

In order to see what the dynamic process model and its theological implications can mean for ministry, we need a framework within which to describe it. As I suggested in Chapter I, Seward Hiltner has provided such a framework in his *Preface to Pastoral Theology*. There he presented his perspectival model for understanding the ministry, in which all the functions of ministry are viewed in terms of the degree to which they reflect the three perspectives of *shepherding, communicating,* and *organizing.* Hiltner insisted that all functions of ministry embody each of the perspectives to some degree, so that compartmentalization of ministry is an abstract fiction.[1] Nevertheless, each function can be viewed from a dominant perspective, which is central to understanding it. Thus the shepherding perspective is usually dominant in pastoral care, the effort of the minister or other representative Christian to meet the personal and spiritual needs of individuals (though this may well be done through groups). The communicating perspective is dominant in preaching, worship, and teaching; and the organizing perspective is dominant in administration, governing, and relating the church to the world.

Though there is some risk in oversimplifying and compartmentalizing the ministry by identifying perspectives with functions, for our purposes this identification can help us to be systematic in viewing it, provided that we keep in mind that such identifications are only partial. We shall, then, look at the functions primarily identified with each perspective to see what the levels of functioning in the salvation-health model mean for them.

Before beginning this discussion, I must note that unless a minister has developed the ability to identify the functional level of those to whom he seeks to minister, including himself, this kind of material is useless at best and quite destructive at worst. With very rare exceptions this kind of ability cannot be developed without special training, often accompanied by individual counseling or psychotherapy. Fortunately, there are now many opportunities for ministers to develop this ability, along with the interpersonal skills and relational competence needed to implement decisions. First and foremost of these is clinical pastoral education, the pioneer development in this field, now well established under the auspices of the National Association for Clinical Pastoral Education in over two hundred centers in the United States, Canada, and overseas. In addition, the newer group training movement offers many opportunities for training in that important area, which also increases sensitivity to individuals.[2] Some denominations are beginning to develop their own programs on a regional basis. Taken all together, these opportunities mean that no minister may any longer excuse himself from developing the necessary abilities, as has been true in the past.

These programs do not use the salvation-health model, but they do provide dynamic understanding which is needed for its use. Ministers who are clinically trained will be able to see the applicability of the model, and to employ it without using it as an intellectual weapon to condemn those whom they don't like and applaud those whom they do like. For this is admittedly a danger with any new approach to understanding people.

2. Shepherding, or Pastoral Care

Level One. In relating helpfully to persons struggling at the level of bare maintenance, ministers need above all to learn "body English." Although words can be helpful at many points, the basic medium of communication is nonverbal. One conveys hope and trust by the way he comes into a sickroom, by his gestures, by his eye contact, more than by words of reassurance, though it is often important to listen and understand, verbally.

This is doubly true when one is ministering to a person seemingly out of touch with other persons, as in shock or a coma. Often in such cases the person is aware, however dimly, of the presence of others, and the valence of this presence makes a great deal of difference to him. He "prehends" whether the persons are really for him in empathy or essentially indifferent or calloused.

This point is not intended as a "technique," for, like other skills, nonverbal communication must be learned (small-group experience of the "encounter" variety can help a great deal). Rather, it is an implication of the basically relational character of life, and of the salvatory potential of even those whose existence seems totally bound by the struggle to survive. The relationships they experience in that struggle may make the crucial difference in its outcome, since we literally participate in the lives of those with whom we relate.

All these things are true as well with the very young, who in their first days and weeks struggle in their own way toward development. The "representative Christians" who relate to

them for the most part are their parents, and in particular
their mothers, who are as truly ministers as those ordained.
Hence the need for them to be warm and empathic, attributes
of mothers which are not automatic, popular mythology to
the contrary.

Level Two. Here the minister's role as a significant adult
supportive figure for children and early adolescents has long
been recognized. What has not been so generally recognized,
however, is that the minister, as the person in the church
charged with the salvation of all its members, young and old,
has an obligation to protect children from expectations that
they will respond like adults able to make responsible decisions on their own to church programs which may be unwittingly exploitative of them. Although children enter often
with enthusiasm into competitive projects from church and
school attendance to fund drives, the associations built up by
these enterprises later will serve as negative blocks against
church participation, or will continue as a base of relating to
the church when more mature modes should be taking their
place.

In direct one-to-one relationships with children, ministers
should be able to be open and concerned in their relationships
with children, who are quick to sense when something is
being covered up. Their development depends upon their
getting both sufficient information and a warmth of response
from significant adults. In times of crisis with children, such
as the death of a parent or grandparent, the minister needs to
give straightforward answers to children's questions, and to
be able to hear their expressions of grief, however disguised.
Often children feel somehow responsible for the death of a
loved one, and need reassurance that this is not the case.
Above all, ministers must keep in mind that credibility has
become a precious commodity in our society, especially in
the communications of adults to the young.

Finally, ministers need to learn to recognize when a child
is in developmental difficulty and to take appropriate steps to

communicate this to the parents and assist them in getting the help the child—or often the whole family—needs. Some work with children in a clinical setting will be of great value in developing this kind of ability. Where the case is clear-cut, usually the parents do see the need, but in many borderline cases they will deny that there is anything wrong, since it is human to do so, or else exaggerate the difficulty if it meets the needs of the family to use the child as a "scapegoat" for problems in the family that touch all its members. This is especially likely to occur in adolescence, where the "normal" patterns of development often entail a certain amount of deviant behavior in terms of the norms of our society. Withdrawal, moodiness, experiments with sexual feelings and with drugs are all a part of growing up in our culture, and can be taken too seriously by parents. On the other hand, it is certainly true that such experimentation can lead to very serious problems, and experience and training are needed to tell the difference.

In all this the minister should keep in mind that the child and adolescent is basically trying to find the patterns of living that are right for him. He is not able to make long-term commitments, and should not be expected to. Life is very real, but it is still very experimental.

✗ *Level Three.* At this level we find probably the majority of adults in most churches. They are maintaining themselves, but by the use of various kinds of compensatory devices of which they unconsciously (and sometimes consciously) fear to let go. Generally, long-term, expressive, insight-oriented counseling or psychotherapy is not indicated for such persons, for this would entail their giving up the compensatory devices. Rather, short-term individual or group counseling which is basically supportive in character is indicated. Such counseling involves the ventilation of feelings and thoughts, giving emotional support, trying to get a picture of the reality situation confronted by the person, interpreting to him what seems appropriate in the light of these factors, and sometimes attempting to change the environment, especially the family environment. Family counseling may also be appropriate in such cases, in which the goal is not to make over the family relational configuration completely, but rather to improve communication and take some of the pressure off some members which is being applied unwittingly by others. Marriage counseling may be done in the same way when only the couple is involved.

Sometimes a person (or a family) who has been living primarily at the compensated maintenance level encounters a severe personal crisis in which the compensatory devices that have been employed are destroyed or severely damaged. In such cases long-term counseling or psychotherapy may be indicated, and the person may be enabled to move upward to another level of functioning. Such a crisis may arise through the loss of a marital partner through death or divorce, job loss, or a change in job "description" like promotion or, in cases of wives supporting husbands through graduate school when schooling is completed, job change, which impairs identity and worth.

An actual case of this kind developed when a widow who had recently lost her husband after being married for more than thirty years came to her pastor, who was an experienced counselor, severely depressed. Her whole life had revolved around her husband, who had dominated and controlled her throughout their marriage. Through extended counseling she was able to drop her compensatory maintenance device of passive submissiveness and begin to develop her personality as an outgoing, autonomous person who had much to offer others and herself through participation in the salvatory process. This case is far from being unique, though it is somewhat unusual for a person with six decades of compensated living behind her—a tribute to both counselor and counselee! [3]

These cases are exceptions, however, since most persons who function at the compensated maintenance level do so because of personality impairment in childhood and youth of sufficient severity to make genuine advancement very difficult for them. Usually the pastor's best strategy is to try to strengthen their compensatory devices, and to help them to use them in such a way as to make them less costly both to themselves and to others. Here we can see a prime instance of why the principle of justification by faith alone is a regulatory, rather than a constituent, principle of our understanding of man in this model. Persons functioning at this level are justified by their "works" which they do through their maintenance devices, and to deprive them of these (or to seek to do so, since they are usually held tenaciously) is to jeopardize their ability to function at all. Yet justification by faith does operate as a regulatory principle, since it may be a genuine goal toward which persons who are on the borderline between Levels Three and Four, and who are struggling to get beyond maintenance to development, and the risks attendant to that level. In such cases it serves as an operational norm needed to assist counselees toward the next level possible for them, though it may or may not be verbalized as such, depending on the total context. As indicated in Chapter IV, Level Four is ordinarily an appropriate level for young adults, and older persons may be able to skip it altogether through counseling or psychotherapy, though this is not always the case.

Persons functioning at Level Three are not always easy to identify, as the quality of their participation may on the surface appear to be freer and more intense than it actually is. By means of personal interviews, however, the essentially brittle quality of their lives will be revealed by the pattern of defenses around the principal compensatory devices. These defenses have been alluded to on p. 119, above. In some cases of panic reaction, the breakdown of defenses is obviously dramatic, and the problem is restricted to getting appropriate help, often from mental health resources in the community, with which every responsible pastor must be familiar.[4]

Level Four. Persons functioning at the level of compensatory development (who are generally young adults, as has been noted) are often good candidates for more intensive forms of counseling and therapy, *when they sense the need for help.* Even more than maintenance-oriented compensators, they are generally resistant to this idea, since it seems to them to pose a threat to their participation and continued development. Often they are right, for development partially as compensation for lack of inner identity and worth is a "normal" part of our cultural pattern, as we have noted. Nevertheless, many young people do need help in finding their way through the complexities of modern life, particularly in the areas of marriage, vocation, and morality (see pp. 103–107, above).

Premarital counseling assumes great importance in the light of these considerations, for it is an opportunity for the minister to explore with the couple their attitudes and feelings toward each other, and to see their implications for the forthcoming marriage. Good premarital counseling may thus occasionally result in the marriage's being called off or postponed, or in the minister's refusal to perform the ceremony. It should lay the groundwork for the couple to come to the minister (or some minister, if they leave his community) for help with their marriage should the need arise. Too much marriage counseling is overly concerned about the "nuts and bolts" of marriage, such as budgets and sex. Not that these are unimportant, but they should not be the central focus of marriage counseling. If attitudes and feelings can be clarified, those matters can be easily dealt with.

If the occasion does arise for marriage counseling, in which the marriage is recent enough still to be in the developmental phase (roughly the first ten years for a young couple), a depth approach emphasizing insight into the personality patterns of the couple may well be in order. Often in such cases the problems arise because the marriage has served its developmental purpose for one or both partners, and has failed to become an "intrinsic" marriage in which the relationship between the couple has itself become paramount. The outcome may or may not result in the continuation of the marriage, but if it is successful it will result in continued development for one or both partners, or in their being able to move beyond the level of compensated maintenance altogether.

Such counseling is best carried out, initially at least, on a mixed-mode basis in which individual interviews are employed as well as conjoint interviews. Later, one or the other modality may be found to be best suited for the couple. In some cases involving very new marriages the counselor soon finds that the difficulty has arisen because there was intrinsic incompatibility from the start, due to extreme neurotic needs on the part of one or both. In these cases referrals for intensive psychotherapy are in order if there are means and motivation. Otherwise, a dissolution of the marriage may well be best, and will often occur anyway.

In all cases of marriage counseling, ministers ought initially to regard instances of "acting out" sexually ouside the marriage as symptoms of difficulty rather than as violations of the moral code. Acting out as a pattern which continues after counseling is well under way is usually a sign of a basic personality disturbance that can best be treated, if at all, by individual, long-term psychotherapy.

Vocational counseling is more obviously related to development than is marriage counseling, but this relationship is in part more apparent than real. Though it is possible to get some genuine knowledge of a young person's aptitudes and interests by means of tests, questionnaires, and interviews, it is not possible to assist him in making a vocational decision that will be necessarily conclusive before he begins his vocation. This is because, as has been noted (see p. 105, above), working at the vocation itself is vital to continued development of one's sense of identity and worth, and when these are relatively secure, the vocation chosen may lose its appeal. Only if the vocation is genuinely "adopted" as one's own in the course of working at it will it continue to be fulfilling. Hence counseling centered on vocation may be needed more than once in the course of a career, even when the best available was engaged in at the outset.

Although vocational counseling is properly the work of specialists when done thoroughly, ministers in the parish and other settings, particularly college and preparatory school chaplains, need to develop basic skills and understanding. Fundamental is the idea that vocation is rooted in the development of personality, and must not be regarded as involving only, or even primarily, narrow skills, aptitudes, and interests. These are important, and can be rather easily determined through the use of a standardized vocational test such as the Strong Vocational Interest Blank. But also crucially related are feelings about parents and siblings, some of which lie well beneath the surface of consciousness. Some of this is related to parental wishes about what career the young person should follow, although these are often not very clear in our age of permissiveness. But much of it is at the deeper level of basic love, hate, and fear coming from early childhood. Some young men consciously choose a vocation that was followed by their fathers (or consciously avoid it), only to fail because of unconscious fear of surpassing, and thereby defeating their fathers. My own experience in counseling with seminary students suggests that this kind of root problem lies behind difficulties of an academic or vocational nature in many more cases than common sense would lead us to believe.

The area of morality is, of course, one in which the "normal" problems in development have been greatly intensified by rapid social change and confusion in the realm of values. Many young people are caught in this maelstrom with certainty only about one thing—that the values of their parents are wrong. They see the hypocrisies of the older generation and abhor them, making it difficult to see also the genuine value in their morality. In this situation all moralizing about sex, alcohol, drugs, and even honesty and truthfulness is bound to produce only more alienation. By moralizing I mean the communication of prohibitions, admonitions, and regulations without giving reasons that are convincing to young people. Such moralizing is appropriate for children, who as we have noted, essentially function with "law and order" morality in any case. But young people must be enabled to move beyond that stage without needing to reject everything in the culture.

Individual pastoral care is not the most effective mode of helping them to do this in many cases, though it may be useful where the young person himself experiences a personal crisis in which values are involved. The minister, like other older persons, is suspect, sometimes especially so in churches in which his role as value bearer for the community is still strong. Hence he is at a disadvantage, initially, at least, no matter how good his intentions and even his skills are. He must be ready to share his position to achieve credibility, but if he does so he may appear to be moralizing, even when he uses language that does not seem coercive.

Group pastoral care with peer groups of young people can be helpful in which the minister or other adults with credibility can participate if they are able to do so genuinely and without the presumption that they really know best. The actual situation today is that no one knows best, for the world is changing too rapidly. Nevertheless, the experiences of older persons can be of great value to the young if they are communicated in such a way as to be heard. Young people trying to find viable life-styles need to know what the models available from the past have been like if they are to fashion models for themselves. Otherwise, they are limited solely to the fads that the youth culture itself develops, which, as Tom Wolfe has taught us, may owe more to the ecology of a drive-in restaurant in Los Angeles than to any considered principles of human conduct.[5]

This approach can be taken also with adolescents who are essentially functioning at Level Two, especially since they are making more and more demands that they, too, be given a

voice in institutional life that affects them directly. This means
that they are serious about their participatory patterns, even
if these may be of less duration than those characteristic of
slightly older youth functioning at Level Four. In fact, mixed
groups of Level Twos and Level Fours may well be a useful
approach, since those who are more genuinely committed to a
participatory pattern can offer a wider spectrum of experience to the less mature Level Twos.

The church is one of the few institutions in our culture in
which persons at different levels of the salvation-health continuum participate, which gives it virtually a unique opportunity for establishing communication between generation and
even decade gaps. Through group pastoral care—which can
best be called "encounter" groups in today's language—this
opportunity can be pursued more than it often has been. All
too frequently the church has simply followed the pattern of
the culture in rather rigidly segregating different age and
interest groups, thus perpetuating, rather than overcoming,
the generation gap.

In concluding this discussion of the pastoral care of Level
Four persons, I think that a word of caution about initiating
relationships is in order. A head-on approach is seldom effective, since the Level Four person is by definition deeply committed to his vocation, his marriage, and his pattern of morality or life-style. He does not readily admit the need for assist-
ance in these areas once the pattern is established, for to do
so is a direct threat to his identity and worth. Hence initiative
should be taken only within a rather firm trust relationship
with the minister, unless the breakdown of the pattern is evident to the person, in which case he may already have begun
a more basic defense at Level Three or even Level One,
where supportive measures are most useful, at least until equilibrium can be reestablished. If initiative can be taken, however, when it appears to the minister that the pattern is not
a viable one, much pain and suffering can be prevented, as
well as loss of salvatory potential. This point underscores the

necessity for the minister to develop a trust relationship with all his parishioners as soon as possible after accepting a new charge.

✗ *Levels Five and Six.* These levels can be treated together because they are both relatively free of compensatory devices, though Level Five is somewhat less so. Pastoral care at these levels is both easier and more difficult. It is easier in the sense that persons functioning at these levels seldom need sustained attention, and when a problem does arise they usually can see it rather clearly themselves and will take the initiative in seeking help before the situation gets out of hand. But since they are often (or should be) leaders in the parish with whom the pastor works closely in the affairs of the church, they for that reason may sometimes find it hard to consult him about personal matters. Hence he needs to be "tuned in" on possible signs of difficulty, such as mild depression or unwonted nervousness or forgetfulness.

As has been noted in Chapter IV, persons living at these high levels of participation are vulnerable to the crises of life just as others are, though somewhat less so. They, too, may have difficulty in adapting themselves to loss of job or spouse, and particularly may be vulnerable to patterns of overwork, which Wayne Oates has aptly termed the "workaholic" syndrome.[6] Since they have such a high potential for salvatory participation, their chief defense when disturbances do arise is often to work all the harder and participate all the more. The pastor's temptation is, of course, to encourage this "workaholic" pattern, since such persons are usually very effective in their contributions to the church. This temptation must be firmly resisted.

Another kind of pastoral care, not crisis-oriented and actually just as closely related to the communicating perspective at points as it is to the shepherding perspective, is what has traditionally been called spiritual direction. At Levels Five and Six spiritual direction is often an appropriate modality, and will, in fact, be sought from the minister. Although such direction has been associated with authoritarian approaches in the past, in which the spiritual director told the person he was directing what to read, how to pray, what to expect in devotional life, and generally interpreted life for him in all its dimensions, in practice it was by no means always such a unilateral affair. Today such an approach is out of the question, except with children to a certain extent, but the essential core of spiritual direction as a relationship within which matters of the spirit are discussed remains a viable pastoral mode, though a much neglected one. In such a relationship the minister can himself continue to develop his own ability to participate. Discussion of Biblical themes will be used as a vehicle in some churches where this is rooted in the tradition, but the process need not be limited to these alone. Generally this most intensely personal form of communication will take its cue from live personal concerns, and for this reason cannot be utilized in groups larger than two or three persons. In larger groups shared problems and questions of a vital nature can be dealt with as we have noted in discussing Levels Three and Four, but at Levels Five and Six this is not the need so much as mind- and spirit-stretching discussion with solid intellectual content.

3. Communicating

I shall not be as detailed in treating the perspectives of communicating and organizing as I was in dealing with pastoral care, which is my own field. This is partly because I have no claim to expertise in these areas, and partly because some of the points already dealt with have relevance also for communicating and organizing, and need only to be mentioned.

Level One. The importance of nonverbal communication at this level has already been discussed and will not be repeated. The verbal aspects of communication most appropriate are those which will reassure and support the person struggling to maintain a bare level of maintenance. For persons familiar with Scripture, readings from the Bible, and in particular from the King James Version with older persons, is still the No. 1 strategy, coupled with prayer for sustaining and healing. In dealing with questions of survival, ministers must communicate what they themselves believe, though not necessarily everything they believe. The important thing is communication of hope, and a hopeful attitude is communicated better by expressing deeply held convictions than traditional doctrines if these are not really held.[7]

Level Two. Here we come to one of the chief controversies in the church. What should be taught to children and young adolescents? There are many factors involved in this question which are beyond the scope of this inquiry, but nevertheless the model being employed should have something to say.

Broadly speaking, it appears to me that there are basically four options open to the churches, though some can be combined to produce more. First, there is what might be called the content approach, which concentrates on giving children and adolescents information about the Bible, the tradition, and to some extent about the contemporary churches. The basic assumption here is that this information will at least provide some basis for making decisions in the religious area later in life. A second approach is that of attempting to teach children directly to be religiously inclined and to live a self-consciously moral life, whether rigidly conformist or socially oriented. Usually the moral development sought is assumed to be dependent upon the religious development, and both are taught by examining various kinds of life situations, some Biblical and some contemporary. The traditional Protestant Sunday school usually combined these two approaches with greatly varying weight toward one or the other. A third option, now enjoying considerable popularity, is to orient religious education around family life, with families worshiping together, studying together, and engaging in other activities together. This approach tries to take advantage of the transmission of values through parents to children by associating this directly to the church. A fourth approach is to offer no religious education at all in the shape of a specific program for children, on the grounds that any such program will inevitably be self-defeating in today's cultural crisis.

The salvation-health model, which views children as participating mostly for the sake of development in rather obvious ways, suggests that the content approach first sketched will not usually be successful because of meaning shifts in the content as the person continues to develop. What is a pleasant story for a child of five (e.g., Noah and the Flood) becomes implausible humbug for an adolescent, who is not placated by being told that the story is really a "true myth," since it was originally represented as literally true. This illustrates the basic difficulty of the content approach. Though it is possible to teach religion in some form to every age, that which is taught earlier will tend to make more sophisticated understandings needed later on difficult to accept on grounds of credibility. Children and young people have a rather direct and literal outlook on life. Black is black and white is white. They are not matters of perspective. When they make it to Level Four or Five, then they may be able to see these matters in perspective, but by then they may well be out of the church altogether.

The second approach may have more to offer to adolescents, provided that the religious and moral emphases do not have the flavor of an imposition of ideas and rules from the past. These will inevitably serve to alienate many, while others who seem initially to endorse them will later find them repugnant when they begin thinking independently. If the program can be worked out on the basis of questions that everyone must ask, rather than answers that must be embraced, then this approach may have a real chance. In no case is this approach really appropriate for children, who are not in a position to ask religious and moral questions except at the level of a "game" they might play for a while.

The third approach utilizing family ties has the built-in problem of the resistance to traditional values that is involved in family relationships generally. Hence it is very problematic as a primary mode of operations, though offering something as a supplement to other approaches.

The fourth alternative of no program seems actually to be best in view of all the circumstances. Children should still participate in some church activities with parents, and resources could be made available to adolescents when they start asking the questions. In these ways the church would be a part of the "life space" of the children and adolescents without the "demand" quality which has all too often been communicated to them in the past. From my point of view they could become communicant members without a great deal of formal didactic instruction which is largely lost or resisted. They would learn by participation what the church is like.

Before advocating the abandonment of the educational program of the church as we have known it, however, I must concede that there are great risks in so doing—risks that the church will completely fail to reach the children for whose nurture it is in some sense responsible.

One recent attempt to restructure the educational approach of the church appears to have promise of overcoming at least to some extent the problems that I have raised. William L. Roberts has proposed that the educational approach to children be remodeled along the lines of supervision in clinical pastoral education. This would mean that the process would deal with questions that the children themselves raised in a personal way (though not abandoning the "content" of the faith either, which could be related to those questions). The ongoing process of supervisory learning could conceivably effect the shift from the "black and white" understanding of children to the more sophisticated approach of adolescents and adults without loss of meaning, since it would hold the interpersonal equation constant while this shift is taking place. Roberts has conducted a pilot study which appears to show

that such an approach has this promise, though it is too limited to tell whether it would be effective over a long span of
time. If this proves to be the case, and Roberts can get his
approach implemented on a wide scale, the position set forth
above of giving up a specific educational approach to children
as a group would have to be modified.[8]

A recent survey conducted among Presbyterian churches in
the Philadelphia area in an effort to determine the causes of
the decline in church school attendance there resulted in the
conclusion that the greatest single factor was the lack of a
sense of "mission" or purpose in the churches showing decline.
A second factor was the lack of interest and involvement of
the pastor in the church school, while formal curriculums
seemed unrelated. These findings do not conclusively support
the contention offered here that no formal school is the best
approach, but they do point to the significance of the church's
total participation in the salvatory process, and to the centrality of the minister's attitudes and role.[9]

Level Three. The primary mode of communication with this
large group of maintenance-oriented people is the regular worship service and the sermon within its context. This means that
whatever other purposes communication in public worship
may serve, it must serve primarily the purpose of supporting
the maintenance patterns of the people who are dependent
upon it to preserve their present level of functioning. This will
appear to be a counsel of defeat to many ministers who have
been seeking to change the attitudes of their parishioners on
such issues as civil rights, racial discrimination, and fair hous-
ing and employment practices. But the failure of many ministers to recognize the centrality of the maintenance function
of worship has led many to attempt attitude change at the
high cost of alienating their parishioners whose deep-seated
maintenance patterns were seriously threatened by the attempts. They failed to recognize that the attitudes of their
parishioners were not merely related to the ideas they enter-
tained, but also to their feelings, many of which were em-
bedded in unconscious conflict.

This does not mean, however, that nothing can be accomplished toward attitude change through worship and preaching. Once the maintenance needs of a congregation are being sufficiently met, then attempts at changing attitudes can be made. In recent years a rather large amount of research on attitude change has become available, and ministers should take the time to acquaint themselves with it. To discuss it here is well beyond the scope of this book, but a good summary can be found in a chapter on "Attitude Change" in M. Brewster Smith's volume entitled *Social Psychology and Human Values*.[10] One salient point that stands out in this research is that values and attitudes are not changed much through any one activity such as preaching, but in combination with other more personally involving modalities it might be quite useful. This usefulness would be enhanced more by focus upon fundamental theological issues that could serve as bridges to reality such as those discussed earlier in this book, rather than an exclusive focus upon the wrongs that need righting—often a direct challenge to personality core defenses. Finally, we may note that the more recent research has tended to emphasize the variety of ways in which attitudes may be related to personality functioning, so that one may hope to effect some changes without necessarily overthrowing, or undercutting, the total personality structure of the attitude holder.

Level Four. At this level the small-group discussion is often effective and can be used in communicating ideas in the areas of vocation, marriage, and morality or life-style, as well as for the more personal emphases of pastoral care oriented groups. The minister himself should be active in these groups whenever possible, though lay experts in these areas can be particularly helpful. Worship forms that resonate with the discussions can both receive ideas from them and make contributions in return.

Levels Five and Six. What was said about pastoral care with these levels in terms of spiritual direction is equally applicable to the communicating perspective. Often persons functioning at these levels can make significant contributions to the Level Four groups also, as well as derive benefits from them.

4. Organizing

In the present crisis of the churches the organizing perspective is probably the most important of the three, so our model must have some relevance here or not really have the significance claimed for it.

Level One. Persons functioning at this level are not by definition able to participate with others except to a quite minimal degree. They can, to be sure, often make significant interpersonal contributions, but not as a part of an organized group, except for the ministry of intercessory prayer in which some can participate.

Rather, the churches need to organize themselves so as much better to meet the needs of Level One persons in their midst by providing lay persons who are capable of giving much with sufficient training in pastoral care to meet these needs effectively. The minister himself should be equipped to give such training, but if he is not, resource persons who can do it are available in most areas, including particularly Chaplain Supervisors of the Association for Clinical Pastoral Education.

Level Two. As noted in the discussion of communicating, organizations of children and adolescents on the church school model has little promise. Much better are attempts to bring them into genuine contact and dialogue with mature members of the congregation in a variety of ways. In all these ways it must be kept in mind that childhood and early adolescence are essentially developmental in character and require opportunities to "try on" various identities without undue commitment to a thing of the past at church-run camps and conferences, but they should be developmental. So also in this day of social action, calls for demonstrations, rallies, peace marches, and various other "crusades" should not be directed to this group, even though many of them will be ready respondents. The Children's Crusade in the Middle Ages stands as a grim and pathetic reminder of the folly of the church in the past in this kind of business.

Organization involving Level Two persons needs to be kept relatively informal, which provides another ground for questioning the generally overorganized youth groups of the present. In addition to providing a vehicle for the spread of the peer group youth culture, these groups also associate the church with the competitive character of our society in their lists of officials and hierarchical executive committees. However much these may be needed to keep adult organizations functioning, in youth organizations they serve primarily as supportive devices for shaky senses of identity and worth which invariably omit those with the shakiest.

Level Three. It is at this level that the implications of the model are most radical. In many churches these are the persons who sit on the official boards of the church in policy-making positions. Inevitably, then, the policies they make reflect compensated maintenance values. Although since in many churches this comes about in part because such persons represent the majority who feel more secure in electing them, much can be done to counter this trend by working toward the selection of Levels Five and Six persons through nominating committees and like bodies. There is much that maintenance-oriented persons can do, in particular in regard to the maintenance of grounds and buildings, and efforts should be made to get them involved in that way. Further, once a policy has been proposed and adopted, they can often be used in its implementation in a variety of ways. Even "radical" policies regarding social issues will not necessarily alienate them, depending upon the depth of their maintenance devices. They frequently will respond to persons whom they admire and respect, also, even when the proposal in question is deeply threatening in some respects. Hence the need to get the person with the highest level of salvation potential in positions of leadership in congregations, for in these persons this potential is usually transparent enough to be identified by all.

On the other hand, Level Three persons will all too frequently respond to "charismatic" figures who seem to be offering them security against threats of humiliation and loss of identity. Hence great effort should be made to keep such persons from positions of leadership and policy-making. People like these usually begin by speaking about preserving "our way of life" and "our faith" and move later to denunciations of all those who presumably threaten them. These charismatic persons are themselves a specialized type of Level Three who have found that they can maintain their own equilibrium only by the extreme measure of gaining the acquiescence of others in their own narrow conception of the world. They may be any age, though twenties and late forties to early fifties seem to be the most likely, as these are the ages in which transitions and development must be made which "charismatic" men cannot accomplish. Hence the person projects his inner uncertainty upon the world and seeks alliance with those with whom this resonates, but who are less articulate. Adolf Hitler was a notoriously successful example of this kind of compensated maintenance person, and more recent examples in public life may readily be brought to mind.

Level Four. In our day, Level Four persons are likely to be questioning in a radical way what they see to be the strictures placed upon them by a maintenance-oriented establishment. This is true in the church as elsewhere. Efforts to persuade them to give up this questioning and accept without question the faith and life-styles of the past are doomed; the viable question is how the churches can best help them to carry on the questioning and protest in the most effective way and at the least cost to themselves and others. In the sections on pastoral care and communicating I have suggested two kinds of small-group approaches to these questions. Now I want to go farther and suggest that the churches must be prepared

to accept the leadership of Level Four people in actively involving them in the struggle for more viable community both
inside and outside the churches. While they are often involved
in these matters more for the sake of their own development
than they realize, their awareness of the issues and alertness
to patterns of restriction put them in the best position for pro-
posing policy and specific lines of action. Though policy-making should ultimately rest in the hands of Levels Five and Six
persons, they should be very attentive to the active Level
Fours, who should also have some direct representation on
official boards. Those not actively involved in social action
may have much to contribute to the development of the worship and community life of the congregation. This would be
particularly true in churches where the small-group life
sketched earlier has become operative.

Though there are dangers that Level Four persons will become so involved with their own particular interests that they
do not see the total context of action clearly and will find themselves caught in situations that are costly to them and others,
it is better for those of us who have an impulse to offer dis-
cretion as the better part of valor to restrain those impulses.
They can use our experience and perspectives, but they do not
need our restraining cautionary advice offered as such. That
is, the risks of restraint are on the whole greater than those of
support, though this does extend to direct violence or provo-
cation to violence. Violence does sometimes have a partially
beneficial effect, but such effects are unpredictable, and violence always has the effect of arousing latent hostile impulses
which may overwhelm the ego. That is, violence is actually
counterdevelopmental, and hence against the main purposes
of those who are committing or provoking it. They become the
chief loser, whoever may benefit, for they will find that their
own development has become truncated.

Levels Five and Six. As already noted, it is from these levels
that the primary leadership of the churches needs to be re-
cruited. This will mean that most of it will be over thirty-five,

and some risks are attendant upon that restriction. These risks can be minimized by listening carefully to younger persons at Levels Two and Four, and are worth it if one can get men and women who are able to participate mainly for the sake of that participation, and not because of hidden personal agenda. I have discussed in Chapter IV the question of how such persons are recognized and shall not repeat it. I need only to stress that some period of acquaintance and observation is needed to discover who is really able to function in such a way that compensation is minimal.

With such persons in leadership roles, the minister can share his professional theology as much as it needs to be shared for effectiveness, without fear that it will be misunderstood or misinterpreted as some kind of controlling and manipulating device. They will be able to see the advantages of such a theology over the best intended "flying by the seat of one's pants," or relying solely upon denomination plan books (which can be useful if not overused). In addition to policy-making, these people are needed for the administrative leadership and direct participation in the various aspects of the church's life which have been discussed.

Realistically, the minister on a new charge may find them in short supply. Instead of organizing prospects into "leadership classes," appropriate pastoral care and referral then indicated is a surer way to develop leaders, since they can be no better than their personalities will allow. Such classes may have their place, however, with leaders who have been selected already and need to learn the "nuts and bolts" of how the church operates.

5. Conclusion

These implications are not offered as a panacea for everything that poses a problem in the parish. Ministers will still need to have the necessary pastoral, communicative, and administrative skills. They will have to learn them from experts in these fields, and to some extent while in seminary, but realistically such skills can be taught in seminaries only in a beginning fashion. Continuing education in them remains a necessity for most.

Underlying this whole book has been a basic commitment to the idea that whatever new forms the church in the future may take, the parish will continue to be focal to its ministry. This is not simply a recognition of the sociological realities of the present, but also of the fact that the parish offers a virtually unique opportunity for the relating of the experiences of persons in all sorts of conditions and levels of functioning. Though it may be modified along federated lines and interests, its basic character offers too much in the way of cross-fertilization to be abandoned altogether.

Further, I have taken an approach that emphasizes the resources which human reason can bring to bear upon the problems of parish life in my insistence that a professional theology is both possible and desirable. It is therefore in order to speak a word in closing about those contemporary theologians who have rejected reason, at least in its historical Western shape, as the key to the renewal of Christianity in our time, and substituted for it the cultivation of festival, fantasy, and a sense of wonder.

Harvey Cox may be taken as a spokesman for this group as an articulate and committed theologian, although in some ways Sam Keen would serve as well.[11] Cox in his *A Feast of Fools* has urged us to recognize the demise of traditional theology in the "death of God" movement and the loss of the sense of transcendence which it represents, and to find in play and fantasy the basic model of the Christian life. By fantasy Cox does not mean withdrawn daydreaming, though he is not against a certain amount of that. Rather, he means "advanced imagining" in which the hold of the world of fact is loosened, and the mind envisions the possibility of worlds far removed from it. Though he does not see the institutional church of the present as capable of nurturing this kind of fantasy in its ritual, which he describes as an "ideological distortion" of true ritual, he does find some elements in the liturgical tradition which might serve as a beginning point. The figure of Christ the Harlequin, who views the sufferings and foibles of mankind with mixed compassion and merriment, is the focus of his attempt at authentic ritual which would celebrate the true comic character of the Christian life and provide for the exercise of fantasy.[12]

Though I obviously disagree with the apparent rejection of reason in his position, I find that in what we are seeking in the life of the Christian and the church we are not far apart. In his term "fantasy" he is aiming at the same experience that I have described as transpropriate, the ability to get beyond the self that one presently has and to enjoy a fresh vision of life. At one point he uses the term "self-transcendence" to refer to his goal for society, which is very close to transpropriate willing as I have employed it, though I have referred to the experience of individuals rather than societies. My suggestion that new forms of worship need to be developed both as means of expression and as contributions to thought and action is another way of putting stress on the need for festival and fantasy.

In short, though I still believe that there is much life in the institutional church which can be aroused by a thinking and responsible professional ministry, I believe with Cox, Keen, and others like them that a new emphasis of fantasy, which can offer "an endless range of future permutations," [13] is likewise needed. But I believe that these are not incompatible emphases, and that the former can provide the structure within which the latter may flourish. For if fantasy is not sufficient for full participation in the salvatory process, it certainly is necessary as the means by which we broaden our vision to futures otherwise unimaginable.

It is precisely because I have a theology in which God is the one who calls man into his future, ever disturbing his attempts to settle for maintenance, that I can affirm the potential creativity of the disruptive but pregnant processes of life in which I find myself. Yet that same theology affirms the continuity of the future with the present and the past, finding in the ages of man's agony and struggle, gladness and singing, the sweat and voice also of God. "Therefore, my beloved, . . . work out your own salvation with fear and trembling; for God is at work in you, both to will and to work for his good pleasure." (Phil. 2:12-13.)

NOTES

1. Seward Hiltner, *Preface to Pastoral Theology* (Abingdon Press, 1958), p. 18.
2. No organization of national stature has emerged as yet in the field of group participation and leadership training, though the new Association for Religion and the Behavioral Sciences gives some promise.
3. This case was used by permission of Rev. W. Burney Overton.
4. The kinds of dramatic breakdown most often encountered are attempted murder or suicide, exhibitionism, voyeurism, and sexual molestation. Less dramatic but no less serious are acute alcoholism, phobic reaction (in which the person is virtually immobilized because of consuming fear of commonplace situations such as streets, buses, or food), and incipient psychoses in which the person is slowly losing contact with reality. In the majority of situations like this the Comprehensive Community Mental Health Centers now operating in many parts of the country are a first line of defense. Where none is yet available the family physician or a psychiatrist known and trusted by the minister should be called. In the case of phobic problems and related forms of distress in which there is a quite prominent focus, such as masturbatory problems, often a behavior modification specialist is the professional of choice to whom the referral should be made. Local councils of community services can usually be helpful in making the best referral.
5. Tom Wolfe, *The Kandy-Kolored Tangerine-Flake Streamline Baby* (Farrar, Straus, Giroux, Inc., 1965).

172 SALVATION AND HEALTH

6. Wayne E. Oates, "On Being a 'Workaholic' (A Serious Jest)," *Pastoral Psychology,* Vol. XIV, No. 187 (Oct., 1968), pp. 16–20.

7. Robert Perske, chaplain at the Kansas Neurological Institute, has written several helpful articles on the subject of the ministry and mental retardation in which discussion of nonverbal communication is presented. For example, see his "The Gap Between the Mentally Retarded and the Pastor: A Case Study of the Gap Between Ministry and People," *Journal of Pastoral Care,* Vol. XXII, No. 3 (Sept., 1968), pp. 160–167.

8. William L. Roberts, "The Supervisory Alternative to the Custodial Contract in the Educational Ministry" (unpublished dissertation, Princeton Theological Seminary, 1970).

9. William E. Chapman, "Why Are Church-School Enrollments Declining?" *Presbyterian Life,* Vol. XXIII, No. 13 (July 1, 1970), pp. 16–17.

10. M. Brewster Smith, *Social Psychology and Human Values* (Aldine Publishing Company, 1969), pp. 82–96.

11. Sam Keen, *Apology for Wonder* (Harper & Row, Publishers, Inc., 1969).

12. Harvey Cox, *A Feast of Fools* (Harvard University Press, 1969), pp. 144 ff.

13. *Ibid.,* p. 18.

Index

Anderson, Herbert E., 79n36
Anthropology, theological, 9, 17, 19, 23, 25, 122 ff.
Apocalyptic, 32, 37

Barth, Karl, 23, 28n15
Browning, Don S., 49 f., 54, 141

Church, crisis in the, 15 ff.
Cobb, John B. Jr., 25, 29n16, 76nn24, 28, 77n30
Communicating, 158 ff.
Compensation, 96 ff., 123
Cox, Harvey, 169 f.

Development, 86 ff., 93 ff., 96, 98, 102 ff., 123
Duncombe, David C., 112, 121n31

Edwards, Jonathan, 20 f., 27n11
Erikson, Erik, 69

Faith, 124 ff.
Forgiveness, 124 ff.

Guilt, 97

Hartshorne, Charles, 11, 25, 58

Health, 9; contemporary conceptions of, 59 ff.; definition of, 71
Hierarchical model, 91 ff., 132
Hiltner, Seward, 10, 13, 17, 19, 27n8, 46, 70, 75n22, 145

Identity, 88 f., 96

Jesus Christ, 35, 36, 37, 38, 54
Jung, Carl G., 65
Justification, 124 ff.; by faith alone, 151

Laing, R. D., 30n16, 93
Lee, Robert E., 113 f.
Loevinger, Jane, 69, 84n61

Maintenance, 86, 88, 91 ff., 96, 98, 122
Marriage, 103 f.
Maslow, Abraham, 110 ff.
May, Rollo, 140n13
Metaphysics, 29n16
Method in theology, 11 ff.
Migliore, Daniel L., 13, 78n35
Morality, 103, 106 f.

Niebuhr, Reinhold, 22 f., 28n15, 137n1

174

Oden, Thomas C., 48 f., 75n19
Ogden, Schubert, 25
Organizing, 164 ff.
Outler, Albert C., 46 f., 73n4

Pannenberg, Wolfhart, 44n10, 55 f., 77nn30, 32
Participation, 86, 89 f., 95, 102, 107 ff., 124
Pastoral care, 147 ff.
Prejudice, 99 ff.
Process philosophy, 24, 29n16
Process theology, 9, 18, 51 ff.; criticisms of, 131 f.
Professional theology, 9, 144 f., 168
Pruyser, Paul W., 10
Psychoanalytic ego psychology, 24, 29n16, 69 f.

Rauschenbusch, Walter, 22
Roberts, David E., 46
Roberts, William L., 161
Resurrection, 32, 33, 38, 44n13

Salvation, 9; in contemporary theology, 51 ff.; definition of, 57–124
Salvation and health, relationship between, 24; in the Old

Testament, 31 ff.; in the New Testament, 31, 35 ff.; in the church to the Reformation, 39 ff.; from the Reformation to the present, 42 f.; in the contemporary situation, 46 ff., 89 ff., 102; schematic model of, 116, 123
Sanctification, 128 f.
Schleiermacher, F. D. E., 21 f., 28n12
Social and political gospel, 131 ff.
Southard, Samuel, 113

Thornton, Edward E., 48
Tillich, Paul, 23, 28n15, 137n1

Violence, 101, 167
Vocational choice, 103, 105 f.

Wesley, John, 20 f., 27nn10, 11
Whitehead, Alfred North, 29n 16, 51 ff., 76nn23, 24, 28, 143n16
Williams, Daniel Day, 11, 25, 47, 74n11, 142n14
Woolman, John, 108 ff., 120nn 19, 24
Worth, 88, 96